HIDDEN MEMORIES

HIDDEN MEMORIES

Best wishes to you, Ken, and to you, Mary.

Enjoy!

by

Edward P. Mihelich

ACKNOWLEDGMENTS

I wish to thank my friends and acquaintances for giving me such continuous encouragement about my writings. I would meet these same people in stores, on the street, coming out of church, and with a smile on their faces, they all asked that same question, "When is all this coming in a book?"

The title and design for my work was created by my wife, Charlene. She has also helped me to proofread my efforts. I am very grateful for her patience, when I was so occupied with my writing, and thereby giving her little time for conversation.

Many personal thanks to my grandniece, Lisa Keyes, for putting all my words in computer form. Keeping a keen eye on a screen requires much perseverance, which she was trained to exercise.

Yes, I am very grateful for being related to a creative family, a wife that is obsessed with music and dance, and nieces and nephews that are gifted with pencil and brush. All sketches and photos have been submitted by the author.

In memory of my professors
and superiors, who have instilled
in me a love for mankind, and
to my parents for blazing so many
trails of joy.

PREFACE

Hidden Memories is a collection of writings, which I have considered as memorable moments given to me during my many interviews with the people of Niles and vicinity. It was so comforting to sit with people who came from all parts of the world, comforting, indeed, to record their many experiences in their course of life. Some of my subjects have already passed from this troubled world, some of whom have become legends in their own right. I have been blessed to have captured their many treasured memories.

Besides talking and being with my characters in their favorite chairs, this book is also about places in our Great Lakes State, that you have undoubtedly heard about, talked about, but have never seen. Perhaps paging through this piece of literature, you will have a better understanding of a state that prides itself on its discovery of iron and copper ore, found deep in the belly of the Upper Peninsula of Michigan.

Finally this publication is about things that you may have never touched or smelled, as you annually traveled in the vicinity of the Straits of Mackinac and particularly the region of Lake Superior, the greatest fresh water lake in the world. My writings have included much of Southwestern Michigan, and being a native of the copper fields, I have covered a vast section of this land of much standing virgin timber, springfed lakes and spring holes, and ageless meandering brooks and creeks, and where the forests abound with wildlife. It is also a place that harbors diverse cultures.

My literary selections comprise the words and thoughts of those who have gained wisdom through years of listening and learning. Many phases of my compositions are also personal in nature, thus making my journeys in this great wonderland more treasured.

So, let's first visit our story tellers and listen to their world. We spend much time with septuagenarians, octogenarians, and nonagenarians, and believe me, what wonders they held in store. We learned about Christmas in European countries. There was so much to digest when we studied about the early missionaries and traders, that used the St. Joseph River as their passage route. Niles, the City of Four Flags, was and still carries the distinction of being a famous railroad center. I was fortunate to have had the opportunity to speak to engineers, conductors, switchmen, yardmen, detectives and railroad clerks.

Leaving this land of much corn, soybean and fruit, we travel to the Straits of Mackinac where some forty years ago, passengers at times perilously crossed this body of water by ferry. Today, the two peninsulas are connected by the Mackinac Bridge.

Finally, our compass now reads West Northwest to the Keweenaw Peninsula, a piece of real estate that projects into Lake Superior. The old-timers have often considered these rocky and treacherous shores as being the graveyard of countless mariners.

TABLE OF CONTENTS

The City of Four Flags

As I told you some weeks ago, Mike Cain, the guardian of the past, gave me some noted literature about Niles' History. Today I wish to share this knowledge with you, though in summarized form.

With the exception of Detroit, St. Ignace and Sault Ste. Marie, Niles is considered one of Michigan's great historic regions. It had been known as the City of Four Flags. The artist George Schultes depicts the countries of Spain, France, England and the United States on the shoulder patch of our local police.

To gain some knowledge of Niles, let's visit the City Hall, which at one time was a mansion given to our city by the late Lowell Chapin on June 3, 1933. It was built in 1882 and owned by Henry and Ruby Chapin. It was indeed an elegant building possessing many wood carvings, cut glass chandeliers and many fireplaces. As you enter the building, you will notice an old grandfather clock, which was once owned by the Geltmacker family, which in German meant "money maker". They were prominent people in Niles living in the area of Front Street where Brenner's junk yard was located. As you gaze about, you will observe a memorial to the Spanish American War Veterans. The field Boulder was given to the city by Bascome Parker. The metal plaque was from the Battleship Main, which sank in Cuban waters on February 15, 1898, and hence the reason for our entry into the war with Spain.

It was through the efforts of Edward Hamilton, once a Congressman in the House of Representatives, that Niles has the distinguished plaque, which was set by some Civil War

Veterans in the old Post Office. When this building was enlarged, the plaque was moved on the City Hall property in 1938. In the left background you will see Ft. St. Joseph Historical Museum. This at one time was the carriage house of the Chapin Estate. For those of you who enjoy Indian lore, the museum has many interesting features about the Sioux Tribe, and other Indian items.

The Chapin Estate was surrounded by a wrought iron fence. The big Parrot Gun that once stood at the old high school is now the City's property. The fence and the Brass Napoleon brass Cannon were saved by the city engineer V.N. Taggett.

It is interesting to note that the oldest Protestant church is the Trinity Episcopal. There were many prominent families that attended this house of worship, one of which was the Lardner family, whose son Ring became a famous author. One of Niles's Junior High Schools was dedicated in honor of its native sons. Mike Cain goes on to elaborate a bit on Lardner, who wrote many plays, songs, was a newspaper man and who later became an editor. He was also somewhat of a cartoonist.

Next door to the Episcopal Church was the Presbyterian Church dedicated in 1916. The original structure was a log cabin building constructed in 1834. Their congregational meetings date back 180 years.

On a hill located on Bond Street, there is a granite cross marking the grave site of Fr. Allouez, a Jesuit Missionary, who undoubtedly once canoed the mighty St. Joseph River. He was born in France and died in the Niles area on August 27, 1689. The Women's Progressive League was responsible for much of Allouez's Memorial.

Fr. Marquette, also a Jesuit Missionary, perhaps knew Allouez, though the former worked with the Chippewas at Sault Ste. Marie, and the latter here among the Potawatomis. It is very possible that they met somewhere on their perilous journeys. Both were natives of France, and without a doubt the Jesuit Order had two of the best missionaries in the Great Lakes Region.

The following is a Four Flags Hotel publication of the historic city of Niles:

Historical soil is this tract of land upon which the city of Niles has been built. Within the present-day boundaries of our city during the 17th and 18th centuries the flags of the four powers were unfurled as they, in turn, took possession of the surrounding territory.

In 1697 the French built a block house and a fort on the east side of St. Joseph River, one mile south of the center of Niles, Michigan. The fort commanded the stream which was navigable by boat or canoe for one hundred and fifty miles from its mouth at the present city of St. Joseph, where it flows into Lake Michigan.

In 1761 the British 60th regiment, then called the Royal Americans, took the block house. The French flag came down and the English ensign went up.

In 1781 the Spanish under Don Eugenio Puree with two great Indian chiefs and tribes surrounded the little block house and fort, and took as prisoners the English soldiers. The Spanish colors were raised. After confiscating all stores and provisions the Spanish burned the fort and eight other buildings, and returned to St. Louis boasting possession of the lands along the St. Joseph River.

In 1783 the Americans through a treaty of peace with the British possessed all the territory extending between the two Great Lakes, Michigan and Huron.

Over this area of ground upon which has been built the city of Niles, Michigan, the French, English, Spanish and American nations unfurled their flags, hence the name, "The Four Flags".

I sat down with Mike a while longer and talked about his life's work, as I wondered how this man gathered so many

3

facts about people, places and things. He told me that at one time he was superintendent of Silverbrook Cemetery for a mere 45 years, as was his grandfather, Arthur Thompson, before him, who worked for 34 years. It was his grandfather really who handed down this information about Niles' residents, both living and dead. There's no doubt, too, that he was abreast of all the local obituaries. Mike also remembers a very frail man, a school teacher by the name of Harry Manfield, who was a great story teller. So, by his reading and meeting with research people, Mr. Cain has absolutely no problem to sit down with you and tell you who's who in this historic City of Four Flags. If you enjoy gathering historical facts about Niles, Mike is our Community's walking encyclopedia!

To conclude our Column for today, I would like to share a letter that George Wyburn sent me the other day that was written by M.D. "Curly" Brown in 1944. It concerned some very strict advice given to his workers at the defense plant, which had been making parts for the Army tanks. W.W.II was still in progress and there was a heavy loss of tanks. This particular building now is the Scoreboard.

M.D. Brown was the president of the shop, and evidently he was getting a lot of static from the top brass about the tank production. Being that he was a very dedicated and conscientious person, and indeed a patriotic one, I couldn't imagine such an individual scheming to burn our country's flag! In his letter he complained about a lack of coordination effort in getting their job done. Mr. Brown was rather blunt when he told his people that wages in this shop come second, and production is first! He may have lost a friend or two when he told them that, but he was very concerned about saving lives across the oceans.

At this point I wonder about the workers, now living, who remember Curly's admonitions. Congratulations on your true spirit.

A Look at Niles in the 20's and 30's

Back again for another look at Niles in the 20s and 30s. Roger Smith of this city sent me practically a research paper about this area. I had a feeling that he was thinking about sending me something for some time now. It looks like he's been reading our Column, so he probably said to himself, "Gee, if Joe can do it, why can't I?" So, here is Mr. Smith's report, and those of you who lived in that era, will know exactly what he's talking about. Sit back now, and enjoy the words of another one of Niles' sages.

You remember when Main Street was surfaced with brick, and on the hot summer days the streets would be watered by a horse drawn water wagon? This was in the 20s and about the same time a city worker would pick up all the litter and horse manure. Can you picture one of your youngsters doing this as part-time work after school today?

There used to be a water reservoir on Main Street south of Hickory - all the waters were piped from Barron Lake with a pumping station along the way.

Some of these accounts may have been recorded in an earlier publication, but another's eye and memory could give us a closer look. Our historian tells us that at one time there was an interurban passenger station somewhere in the vicinity of 2nd and Main and later on Sycamore. There was a shoe shop that was just adjacent to the Main Street Bridge. "I remember taking my shoes to the cobbler there", Roger states. He talked about Kerr's Hardware Store, the Louis and Snell Bank and one of the early A&P establishments. He also stated that the car license bureau was in the J.C. Penney Company building. The first Oldsmobile dealership was Sholtey's, which later became Sears just across the street from Majerick's.

Did you enjoy 3rd Street as your route to South Bend? That's what it was back then. Frazee's Ford was on the NW corner of Cedar and 2nd, then came the A&P and eventually Wonderland.

There was a coal yard along the River between Broadway and Main, also a jewelry, a poultry market, a pool hall and a used furniture store.

The 5th Street Viaduct, one of Niles' first bridges, was made out of wood planking which was periodically replaced because of the heavy pounding of automobile traffic. Roger was quite proud to state that he worked at the mill that produced these planks at Milton Township. Some of the pilings, which the mill also made, were used at the Bertrand Bridge. "I was part of the horse and wagon crew that hauled these pilings", Roger writes. He went on to say that there was a freight house near Wayne Street, through which a sidetrack ran.

Some of our retired local police would probably remember a 'police booth' that was by the viaduct, which was a direct communication line to the downtown gendarmes.

The farmers of rural Niles knew where harnesses were repaired - directly behind the Johnson and Johnson shoe store. The farmers also remember coming into town on a Saturday night to do some shopping or attend a movie. There was angle parking at the time from 5th Street to the Big St. Joe.

Mr. Smith gave me a very detailed report, but I chose to give you the principal physical appearances of this railroad town. Perhaps the Michigan Wire Goods Company, where the present Highrise stands will flash before you, or the Hydes Flour and Gristmill and coal yard on the east side of Front Street between Howard and Ferry Streets will make you say, "Oh, yeah, I remember those places."

The railroad depot for the C.C.C. and St. L railway tracks was located where the present Niles Fishery was at one time located. This railroad breezed through Beebe's Farm and then continued on to Granger, Elkhart and points beyond.

Roger finished his composition by telling us about the 3 level railroad bridge. The middle level was the Airline Railroad, a system that traveled to South Bend, Cassopolis, Vandalia and on to Jackson, Michigan. Now do you know why Niles was and still is called the Railroad City?

BROADWAY BRIDGE IN 1949

Jack Renner sent me some photos of the construction of this bridge. As I studied them, I didn't notice any 'sidewalk supervisors' around, which usually is the case when something is being built. But here are some of the things that I noticed. You could see the old super structure, some of the steel girders, and other parts dangling in the river's current. I am not able to tell you at this moment where the traffic was rerouted, but a catwalk for pedestrians was clearly visible, as were the caissons upon which the bridge was being built. There were several pilings hugging the shores of the river, probably used for reinforcements. Most of the scenes were pictured looking east toward the Niles Police Station.

I am indeed grateful to Jack and Roger for their contributions, and I know that what they had shown and told, will bring some happy moments to the old as well as the young.

Back in the 30s and 40s

I personally did not know your city back then, though I distinctly remember stopping at your busy train depot in 1939 while en route to Detroit on the Twilight Limited. Little did I know that Niles would become the place where I would raise my family. Who would have guessed that the Niles Depot was going to become the subject of motion pictures?

It was in the early 60s that I began molding characters in many classrooms. It was at this time, too, that I became acquainted with the ways and byways of this great railroad town. You might say that it is a part of me now.

The other day I had the good fortune of seeing some classic photos of Niles back in the late 30s and early 40s. These pictures were truly remarkable, and I am sure that they would have moved you, especially if you were a native of this area. Bill Bauernfeind called me over to look at some pictures. What I saw was indeed well worth my visit. The owner of these spectacular shots is Bob Parker. It really gives me much pleasure to be able to tell you in words about your city, and in doing so, maybe it will put a smile on your face, and perhaps incite you to exchange some thoughts with your relative, your friend and your neighbor, too, just like they used to do, that "over the fence talk".

It's rather unfortunate that the Malls took over our cities, as your town looked so thriving with all those stores and the sturdy good-looking automobiles parked along Main Street. I spotted a few Fords and Dodges whose steel looked like the plates of a ship! The town's lamp posts were towering and impressive. At this writing, I will give you the name of the business places, and what may have transpired while you walked the streets of Niles, let's say back in '38 and '41.

Of course, who can forget J.C. Penney's with its double entrance? I gather it was one of your city's best. I'm sure you could go back that far and pick out who your favorite clerk was in that store, and maybe you could also remember the one you deliberately avoided, because she was a crab! It seems you chose Penney's because their merchandise was more suitable, but there were others in your block who thought otherwise.

How popular LaFlor's Grocery Store was back then, I couldn't say. Since you were downtown shopping, it was rather handy though to have a grocer nearby. Chapel's Jewelry was right there, do you remember that? The best dime store without a doubt was Woolworth's, which I noticed had two entrances also. With all these Waldorf's appearances, no wonder this was a bustling and hustling place to shop.

Montgomery Ward I did not see, as that was around the corner. People tell me though, that this was the squeakiest place in town. Remember those floors. There was one like that back in my hometown in the U.P. Everybody knew where the best ice cream was sold. I imagine that during the summer months Thomas Ice Cream Parlor was like a beehive. I pictured parents with their crying children strolling in and out of this sweet shop. Sometimes their ice cream scoops were too hard to handle, and those special flavors would plop on the sidewalk, then the fur started to fly!

Not too many people care for dentists. I did see Dr. D.C. Walter's place, which was located upstairs from the Niles Federal Savings and Loan Building, where you banked your meager savings and applied for a loan. I barely recognized Andy's down the street, and to this day I wondered why this once thriving business ever folded.

You might have known that all this while I pictured people of all walks of life fifty years ago, laughing, chatting, looking. You let your purse dangle from your arm, as you knew it was safe to walk with it in full view. If you had a car, you wouldn't bother locking it, or did you? You didn't bother locking your house either when you left. As I continued on my imaginary trip, I couldn't help seeing two older men, one wearing a cap, the other a hat, one smoking a cigarette, the other his favorite briar. They talked about their grandchildren, their field crops, their fishing hole, or they may have been planning their deer hunting trip.

You needed some hardware for your do-it-yourself project, so you stopped at Kerr's Hardware. While you were there, you couldn't get away from that one compulsive talker. Doesn't that make your day? It was the time of day when the sun was the highest and hottest, so you stopped in at a small restaurant where they sold draft beer. One good mug full did the trick, and while you were sipping, you heard some patrons arguing about religion and politics, and the ones that talked the loudest and the longest were the losers! I spent close to an hour reviewing these outstanding photographs with "Dollar Bill" and his buddy, a baseball card fiend. Being raised in a small Upper Peninsula town of Calumet, I didn't realize that another town and its people could fascinate me that much. I still like to be called the man from the Big Snow Country!

All About Niles' Railroads

I believe it would be most appropriate that during this Centennial of the Niles Depot, that we also tell you about the people that serviced the locomotives, and about the engineers and conductors that guided your route to Chicago and Detroit.

Even before I moved to Niles in the early 60s, I was told that Niles was quite a railroad town, noted for its freight yards and certainly for its passengers. Michigan Central became a big name back in 1892, and it was then that the first passenger train came to this early Four Flags City. And since then, it is still making headlines in the Movie World, in movies, such as the Continental Divide, Midnight Run and Only the Lonely.

It's very likely that people from all parts of our country rode the Michigan Central rails, just to see the depot's grounds, which were adorned with spectacular flowers, hence the name given as also the Garden City.

Just two weeks ago or so, we talked about train sets, scale models, that is, which gave me an idea to talk about the real thing that we have in our city, namely, an outstanding depot and a railroad system that goes back many many years. Imagine tiny trains giving me thoughts about smoke and steam, and this is precisely what it did. I thought of the many engines getting ready to leave the station, when suddenly huge billows of smoke would shoot out of the stack, and the steam would hiss and spurt from the belly of this gigantic machine.

Perhaps the first hint of my telling you about steam and locomotives was recorded in the Niles Daily Star on May 23, 1990. I was fortunate to have met Charles Waldron, as it was

11

he who told me about his father-in-law, Ralph Burdue, who was a boilermaker for the railroad in the 20s and 30s. Since then, I have spoken to several railroad people, who have given me a better understanding about Niles, the ever famous whistle stop.

I have always been thrilled to listen to a train whistle, especially when you know that it's coming from miles away, and especially if it was three o'clock in the morning. From your location, you could almost guess the crossing for which the whistle was blown. And if you listened more attentively, and if you were one of the railroad men, you knew who the engineer was on that freight or passenger train. I guess this was just a little something to pass the time. I believe Art Coleman knows what I am talking about and about whom.

All freight trains had detectives or railroad policemen, one of whom I knew personally. I met Louie Peters in the late 50s, while he was vacationing in the Upper Peninsula. His stories about hobos coming in and going out of Niles were always hilarious. It seems that each time he started to tell me a story, he'd say, "Let me tell ya somethin', Ed." I truly enjoyed and still miss this man's company. His daughter and son-in-law told me about another policeman, by the name of John 'Humpy' Bachman, a tough one, by the way. I wish I knew how he handled those tramps. Should I hear anything more about these men, you'll read about it.

I wonder why it is when railroad guys get together, they have that certain lingo. This brings to mind the talk of my brother-in-law, who at one time used to work for the Milwaukee Road. Since he was a conductor, he would invariably say, while pulling out his watch, "Well, I've got to get goin' now, No. 341's comin' in at 4:10." I believe this must have been some form of dedication, don't you think? I wonder what those railroad cops would say, when they were getting ready to hit the beat?

I wouldn't wonder if that smoke from those hefty engines sometimes covered this town with cinders and soot. Sometimes this nostalgia gets to me, especially when I see a train, and certainly when I hear its whistle. For some, it is just a thing that you have to wait for at a crossing, and for others it continues to be a moving marvel.

Within the last few weeks, I've had some interesting parleys with many dedicated railroad men. I have found out that they have worked hard over the years, and are now enjoying the fruits of their labor. There are still those who patiently wait to punch the clock for the last time. While talking with just a part of the working force, I knew that it had to take a crew of responsible men to put all steam locomotives to work efficiently.

I often think of the section men, often called the gandy dancers, who worked on rails and roadbeds in the heat of the noonday sun. How this name came to be is a mystery to me.

I knew something about the operation of a railroad, but it didn't take me too long to find out how little I knew. I met so many nice guys and they told me about other nice guys, some living, others deceased. They told me that it took a lot of men to operate a railroad system, such as, machinists, firemen, switchmen, brakemen, boilermakers, airmen, section crew, station attendants, trainmaster, yard master, yard clerks, freight and passenger engineers, also conductors, electricians and policemen. This is quite a litany. If I have forgotten your position in this worthy occupation, please bear with me.

In my last week's, column I told you that I've been doin' a lot of parleying with some important people, the ones that kept our trains moving. I consider myself a lucky man in getting some authentic information about railroads in Niles, even though it may have taken some bloodhound heroics. At the end I found my quarry.

Let's begin at the confines of Riveridge Manor. I was told about this old timer as being the oldest living retiree in this area. It didn't take me too long to find Charles Hedstrom. I really get carried away when I talk to someone that's pushing a hundred. This lanky Swede is ninety-eight, and what a memory! I found him sitting in his favorite recliner, listening to the radio, which was nicely nestled on his lap. At that age, he could have been catnapping, too.

He told me he was an offspring of Swedish immigrants. His birthday is June 13, 1894, doesn't that sound like an old old book? When he was two and a half, he and his mother returned to Sweden after the father had died. They had a little farm with a few animals, and when he was nearing twenty, he decided to come back to America. This man impressed me for some reason, maybe it's because he reminded me of the Swedish immigrants back in the Copper Country. I told you that he was lanky, and I meant every word of it. He looked that way in a sitting position, and then I pictured him in a standing posture. If you watched Team Sweden play the Americans in hockey, then you know what I'm talking about.

At this beautiful age, we know that his body may have been spent and bent, but his mind was remarkably keen. His talk was slow and deliberate, but most interesting and informative. He began his railroad career on December 31, 1915. His first job was clerking for a measly dollar a day. He emphasized his stint as a fireman, shoveling coal, sometimes 17 tons of it, on his many excursions to Chicago and Detroit. Besides this, he had to carry water and tend to the signals. He was promoted to being engineer, and there were many sad days on these runs, especially after the invention of the automobile. He said, "it would hurt me, when we would plow into these cars, knowing that people were in them." You see, back in those days, railroad crossings were scarce. He also mentioned that people would take their own lives by lying on the tracks.

14

He brought up the sinking of the Titanic, as he landed in America six days ahead of the disaster. He remembered his steamer, The Baltic. This all sounds so terrifying. Charles Hedstrom enjoyed his life with the railroad. One more thing about this figure. I asked him, "Do you speak Swedish?" He gave me a grin and said, "Yah, oh sure!"

There was another old sage sitting and relaxing in the vestibule of this nursing home, and found out, that he, too, worked for the railroad. He was Hedstrom's junior, as his birthday reads June 12, 1900, and hails from Cadillac, Michigan. As an infant, he became seriously ill, and at which time he was taken care of by his grandparents at Decatur. He came to Niles in 1920, and this is when he became a full-fledged employee of the Michigan Central. Neal Oaks was a switch tender, but he spent most of his working days in the Niles Yard making up trains. It was obvious that both gentlemen were well taken care of in their present home.

Another keeper of the flame was Paul Phillips, who gave forty-three years of his life to the railroad hierarchy. He remembers back in '38, when he started shoveling cinders for $.48 an hour. He was also a fireman, and eventually became an engineer. He and his father, Tom, worked together at times. He gave me a pretty clear picture of freights and passenger trains going around curves on some of those roadbeds. Sheep herds crossing tracks while the train was in motion bothered him the most, as their wool would easily derail a locomotive. Paul retired from the force in '79, and is presently waiting for some warmer weather, and trips to this favorite fishing lakes. At one point in his life, he enjoyed his days behind the yoke of a plane.

Max Young is the next older retiree, who remembers the exact date of his hire, which was March 12, 1928. That's the day he first grabbed a coal shovel and started unloading hoppers. But before that, he worked with a road construction crew, building Highway 60. He was only sixteen then. He was born in the vicinity of Korn Road and Kenzie Creek. He told me a lot of railroad stuff, first about trains running by Barron Lake territory. He pointed out some old roadbeds by his house. Besides unloading coal, he took care of clinkers, dumped fire out of engines, and also lubricated them, worked on the turn tables, made fire in engines, greased drive-rods, took care of the boileroom and ended up as railroad electrician. I guess Max never changed from his outdoor environment, as he's pretty proud of his Arctic Cat. It was he and his snowmobile group that helped many stranded people in the big snowstorm we had back in '78. Our family and neighbors remember that day very well. Even at his age, he is a jack of many trades. His last workday was December 31, 1974.

This is the final chapter of my account of the Railroad Centennial of this city. There is so much pride shown on the faces of the people that have truly made your town the Railroad City. They are indeed a happy lot, and when you see them, but more so, when you hear them, one will come to know that they are somebody special. Just being with them is the best railroad research.

Back in the early days of steam, they say that there were fifty-two sets of passenger trains, twenty-six going west and twenty-six going east. The most prominent of which were the Twilight Limited, the Mercury, the Wolverine, the 20th Century, and the Broadway Limited. When the University Notre Dame had its home football games, there were additional trains put in service.

Many of the retirees talk about the Railroad Hump, a special place where a freight train was made up, sometimes comprising 78 to 100 cars, with freight clerks checking the box cars, gondolas, tanks and flat-cars for their numbers and contents. The railroad people often brought up the Roundhouse the Terminal Building, the many business offices, the repair and machine shops. Today, we see scars of what once was a thriving business. The great Niles Railroad Yard is now in Elkhart, Indiana.

I had the occasion to talk to one of the old timers in the rail business, and he told me a story about the time he lived in Maryland, where he worked on the railroad. He recalls the time where the Roundhouse was located just across the way from a prison, and each time the lights would dim, all the workers knew that someone was being put to death in the electric chair. This same person told me about the many places that railroad employees would meet. Besides Kugler's and Club 66, both famed for their food, there were other places with more noise and camaraderie, such as Ben Kaiser's, the Rainbow, the Stein, and I am sure that spirits would flow elsewhere.

I am especially pleased to give you a list of employees, who are currently working for the Railroad, those who are retired, and those that have worked part-time for the System. In this list, we have a father-son team and many relatives. Let's begin with Pat and Bill Welsh, Al and Ed Selent, Lee Vetterly and son, Tom and Paul Phillips, Earl Sebastian Bachman, and Earl Arthur, Art Coleman, Roy and Art Hall, Brothers Dan and Wally Hickerson, Archie and Dave Phillips, Jim and George Tickfer, and finally, the Gillespie clan comprising Andrew, William, William Sr. and William Jr. Practically all of the above were engineers.

Before we go into another litany of trainmen, I would like to tell our readers that in years past, all operating employees had to wear pocket watches, which were periodically checked for their accuracy by Paul Thayer, the local jeweler.

Now let's tackle the names of the retired engineers of this Rail City: Charles Hedstrom, Ray Kraft, Don Feallock, Gene Brockway, Paul Hahn, Al Selent, John Forler, Dick Borsos, Paul Phillips, Jim Campbell, Cliff Shell, Bill Gillespie, Bill Huber, John Sayne, Paul Mansfield, Morris Kelso, Frank

Cox, Shelby Palmer, Bob Kennedy, Ralph Haynes and Chuck Bailey.

The engineers still on the job include Ed Kimiecik, Arden Reiter, Frank Henegardner, Frank Corothers, Ed Selent, Mike Woods, Bill Gillespie, Jr., George Fletcher, Kelly Patrick, and Lee Patrick.

The retired road conductors now enjoying the fruits of their labor are Lee Vetterly, John Reetz, Roger Beckman, John Beckman, Fred Meyers, Hecter Brown, Manly Curtis, C.W. Smith, Walt Glaser, Ralph Hetler, Bob Prenkert, Jim Crouch, Chuck Adams, Jack Knoll, Bill Bauner, Jim Barkman, Jim Gallager, Jack Wetzel, Jr., Wally Meyers, Ed Smith, Ted Weinke, O.B. Fox, L.D. Ramsby, Chuck Rohde, L.W. Blank, Bill Welsh, Tom Kennedy, Don Wallace, Bill Gombosi, Bob Daron, Jim and George Tickfer, Dom. Saratore, Jim Saratore, Phil Molica, Adam Robertson, Neal Oaks, Ted Reid, Earl Koontz, Garland Chilson, Lyle Dohse, Louie Teeters, L. Barnes, M. Young and J.M. Harrell. Conductors still working are John Yelape, Gene Hansen, Jim Pinkerton, Jim Lintz and H. Ritter. The names of Roger Maddox, Bob Lugger, Bob Meader, Russ Lange, E. Thompson, and Frank Shearer were also brought to my attention.

It is only fitting that we bring to mind those that have already run their race in life, namely, Pat Welsh, Andrew Gillespie, William Gillespie, Earl Bachman and Son Earl Jr., Chuck McCrory and son William, Robert Messner, Joe Barron, Louis Peters, John Bachman, and Robert Weaver.

It is my hope, that all my listings are complete, and should there be any omissions, please accept my apologies.

This being the Centennial year, the ticket agents also need be recognized, namely, of happy memory, Robert Messner, also the names of Betty Ford, Kent Cooper, Larry Highfill, Pam Hagerman, Dave Hageman and Patti Gowanlock.

The Niles Depot and employees of Michigan Central, New York and Penn Central, Conrail and Amtrak have unquestionably left the people of Niles a legacy of countless miles of happy memories. May all of us congratulate you.

A sight to behold!

The Pioneer Veterinarian

People have been asking me, "Have you ever stopped at Doc Fraser's for a story?" This was on my mind for several months, and finally I set my compass to read Redfield East. I had the number of his residence with me, as I believe this was my first trip in this part of Cass County. I knew that once I passed Ironwood, I would have to look a bit more carefully. I spotted a horse grazing in a small pasture, which told me something. As I turned into the driveway, the animal raised its head, and if it had the faculty to speak, it probably would have said, "Yes, he's in ."

The distance from the highway to the house was roughly 500 feet, kind of a winding driveway, giving evidence that the owner loved animals and the outdoors. When I left the car, there was a strong beautiful smell of freshly split hardwood. There were piles of it practically surrounding the house.

The man of animal medicine met me at the door, as he knew that I would be there in a half hour or so. I could see that this was a home, not just a house. One of the first things I asked him was, "Have you used your wood stove yet?" His answer was quick, "You bet!" I believe there were a few nights that week that smoke and vapor trails were coming out of people's chimneys.

'Ol Doc Fraser was a city slicker once, hailing from Highland Park, Michigan. He told me that when he was just a kid, he was crazy about animals, especially dogs. I guess after high school, his father wanted him to be an aeronautical engineer, but the calculus bit was too difficult for him. It could be that when the family moved to a farm, he attended several dog shows, and I believe this is what prompted him to become a veterinarian, and while in college, he lived in a fraternity home, half of which housed vet undergraduates, and the other half was agricultural students. He liked this setup very much. He studied at Michigan State University, which back in the 30s was called Michigan Agricultural College. Of course, you know that today it is a large city in itself.

After receiving his degree, the family moved from Yale, Michigan to Niles on the corner of Fort and Third Streets, which then was in the vicinity of the Mushroom Plant. This is where he started his first business in 1935. Since this was in the Depression Era, I'm sure that his family sacrificed things to help him attain his goal.

In this business of veterinary medicine, he was preceded by Dr. Clemo, and undoubtedly it was he who paved the way for Doc Fraser's success. It was rather amusing to hear him say many of his clients took him to be too young to be a doctor, so he started growing a mustache, which made him look older and more distinguished. He was only twenty-two at the time, and as so many of us are prone to say, "A lot of water has gone under the bridge!"

Both Dr. Graham and Dr. Fraser were the first to start The Michiana Association of Veterinarians. Prior to this organization, animal medicine became rather competitive, and because of this, there was a little animosity among the vets.

As a novice, he recalls his first call outside of town, and that being at the home of John Medo, where he administered medicine to an abscessed cow and a horse with hoof disease. In 1950, he began his practice of cattle insemination. He told me that in the 60s there was a sleeping sickness epidemic with horses, and there were also many cases of dog rabies. Since the introduction of vaccinations, his practice of veterinary medicine became more simplified. In 1953, he became State President of this skilled profession.

Naturally, we got into the subject of today's schooling and that of way back when he attended. He did emphasize that the teachers were strict, and at the same time there was love toward each student. He certainly had a good word for the students that worked with him and for him. He said, "They were good and responsible people, and many of whom began their studies in animal medicine. He left me with this bit of advice for those who wish to embrace this profession. First, a love for animals, a good attitude toward people, and certainly willing to work. All aspirants will undergo a five year course in this study, persevering in anatomy, biochemistry and chemistry, and would you believe, Latin, and this put a smile on my face. With this in mind, I hope that this will change the thinking of many people, that Latin is still very much alive!

This learned man of 47 years of veterinary medicine told me about a worker that was with him for twelve years. He was a warm person, a quiet man, a man who not only loved animals, but also people, and the doctor was so grateful for his presence, as it was he who made his business flourish.

Because of publication restrictions, and because I have so much more to relate, I will try to shorten my account, and yet be informative. Dr. Fraser trained trotting horses, and some of which were winners. It was he who built the Sandy Lane Golf course. Before I end this narrative, I must tell you about some skunks. Back in the 40s, there was a farmer in the vicinity, who gave the doctor a litter of five skunk kits. He asked the doctor to descent one for a pet. The favor was granted. The remaining four kits were also descented, which he gave away or sold for a small fee, as it took some doing for this operation. The Law stepped in and a penalty had to be satisfied. Evidently, our physician wasn't aware that wild animals could not be kept as pets without special permission.

It was indeed a pleasure talking to this man. My only regret was that I didn't meet Mrs. Fraser, who gave birth to eight children, and who is now deceased.

Dr. Bonine, The Philanthropist

I enjoy using superlatives when describing people. In the past, I have given names to individuals because of their derivations, and for some, I have given titles because of their excellence in life.

Our next most prominent figure in Niles' History was Dr. Fred N. Bonine. I have heard his name mentioned so many many times by my spouse, a native of this city, but also by countless others in Berrien County.

This City of Four Flags has the distinction of harboring some very important people. I am sure that our older readers may have brushed shoulders with the following personages, and if they had not, they perhaps wished that this was so. At any rate, the names of the Dodge Brothers, John and Horace, of automotive fame will be remembered, and then the squeaky floors of the Ward Family, and next reading the captions of Ring Lardner, and of course, the greatest of the sons of Niles was Fred N. Bonine.

He was a world famed ophthalmologist, which to the local Indians meant, "The One Who Brings Sunlight." His father, Dr. Ivan J. Bonine, served in the Civil War as a medical surgeon. After the war, the older Bonine became a conscientious politician. His son Fred also studied medicine, and he, too, became an avid statesman. Besides his prolific work as eye doctor, he was mayor of our city for three terms. All these great achievements took place in 1900.

This young French Huguenot studied his medicine at the University of Michigan. While he was there, he held one of the world's dash records. Because of his unusual academic abilities, he furthered his studies in London and Paris. They

24

say that he was quite a sportsman, and loved his special horse named F.N.B.

He was indeed a specialist in his field, and an outstanding humanitarian. He was known throughout the world, as his patients were not only local or from the States, but also from abroad. Thousands sought his miraculous remedies.

Those of you who are familiar with the Old Michigan Central Railroad Depot, it was there that his friends, the railroad people, would put up signs telling the passengers headed for Bonine's Office, that "he won't be in today" thus saving them an empty trip. Can you feature a man of such renown? His Office was down on Fifth and Main second floor. No doubt you can still picture hundreds of people waiting to see this specialist, waiting upstairs, on the staircase and on the sidewalk, something like buying tickets to a World Series! Records show that there were times when he would take care of two hundred patients a day. His biggest "enrollment" was five hundred. His Office Fee was two dollars for the first visit, and one dollar thereafter. He often had trouble collecting monies that people owed him. He didn't fret about it though, and there were times that he would take care of his patients gratis.

This philanthropist was a tall and gentle man with prominent physical features. Any Civil War Vet that walked in for treatment wasn't charged a penny if he could tell the doctor some war story about Gettysburg! Usually every patient sat in the Old Rockin' Chair.

Mike Cain, our happy historical wanderer, told me a little something of Bonine's personal garage. On it, he had fastened a large airplane propeller, and of what significance it had, Mike couldn't say. Now, who else could have come up with this little tidbit, if not Mr. Cain?

Dr. Bonine was very well liked and respected, especially by the railroad people, who had the misfortune of getting pieces of cinder or metal in their eyes. They knew that they would receive instant care.

The Ringside was the Doctor's favorite pastime, and if he knew that Jack Demsey was fighting that day, he'd be there. He and Jack were pretty close, and Jack eventually became his patient.

It's been a half a century since this renowned physician died, and I know that there isn't a day that someone, somewhere doesn't talk about this healer of man.

The Hilderbrand Hotel was a busy place back then, one of the better eateries in town. Who should be one of its steady customers, if not Dr. Bonine. I remember interviewing Eunice Stephens about a year ago, when she told me that she waited on the Doctor while she was a waitress at the Hotel. She was called "Little Stevie", and she had the distinction of putting out the street lights at dawn!

Roger Lorenzen, The Propeller Man

It just doesn't seem proper that after one has run his course in life, that his knowledge be left unheeded. There are many such men and women, by whose graves we stand, read and meditate, "If I had only stopped a moment to talk and listen to their words of wisdom." I find it so gratifying when I can sit with our senior citizens and record their many episodes in life. It's comforting to know when they tell me that they enjoy my accounts of their city or about some special person. I will invariably hear them say, "Oh, I could have told you more about that."

I've been waiting for some time to interview today's subjects, and I found them to be most interesting and captivating people. It is indeed exhilarating when they tell you that they have reached the 80 mark or thereabouts. Both Roger and Mary Lorenzen are like "open books". After our brief introductions, Roger took over the reins. He was so deliberate and precise with his thoughts, and I made it my business to be as accurate as possible with all my information. He told me that he was of German descent coming from Atlantic, Iowa, a small city in the southwestern part of the State. His father was a telegraph operator for the Rock Island Railroad. At age 14, he worked for the Western Union when he was busy making deliveries on his bicycle after school and on weekends. When he graduated from high school at 18, he joined the Heath Airplane Company in Chicago, and helped build the famous Heath Baby Bullet Racing Plane, which was propelled by a 33 horsepowered engine. Making propellers was his specialty. This was in 1928, and he's been doing it ever since. Only engineers know how to make propellers!

Back in Iowa, he remembers making Gliders. We sat and talked quite a while, and now it was time for "show and tell". He left the room and told me that he would be right back. I could hear him in one of the adjacent rooms gathering material for the "show".

It was Mary's turn now to tell me about her lineage. Her father was an Englishman from the ol' sod, an artist, I might add. She did state that she had wished that someone would have encouraged her to pursue some form of art work, as she enjoyed painting very much. Her father was an important figure at the Niles National Printing Company. I believe he was the head lithographer. Just before Roger returned, Mary told me about her father's associations with Ed Hodgson, another one of Niles' early pioneers. He came here from the East bringing with him some oxen used to clear land for his homestead. I guess he and Mary's father became close friends, and being that Ed was the senior, he had many stories to tell. Ed and Mary's father spent countless summer nights visiting each other on their porches smoking their pipes, and watching the U.S. Satellite Echo flying across the sky until it disappeared. Many times they wouldn't say a word until the Echo's return, and I suppose that it would be at this time that either one or the other would spit over the railing of the porch. Incidentally, they both had hearing problems.

I could see that Roger was anxiously waiting for his turn to continue with his prolific story. He showed me some enlarged pictures of himself as a Western Union messenger, and some classic photos of those racing machines. He left the hardware for the last, as this is when he showed me a valve that he created back during W.W.II. It was used to regulate the pressure of an airplane's cabin. At the time, he was doing sub-contract work for General Electric. Next came his pride and joy, his hand carved propellers. Believe me, these were not "store bought". This was Mr. Lorenzen's work! You might have guessed that his smile told the whole story. Just to watch him explain the function of a propeller, gave me some idea of what a good teacher can do even in times like these. Since his shop was located by the Niles City Airport, he often brushed shoulders with my brother-in-law, John Miswick, who was a pilot in the 50s and 60s until he was grounded because of ill health.

I'm sure that most of you are familiar with the name of Robert L. Ripley's column Believe It Or Not! It so happens that Roger's name was recorded in this Column some years back. Since it is of worthy note, I will give it to you verbatim. "Roger E. Lorenzen has carved over 3500 commercial airplane propellers out of birch wood by hand - including the world's largest wood propeller 16 feet long weighed 194 lbs. whittled from laminated block weighing 550 lbs.

When the Heath Airplane Manufacturing Company from Chicago moved to Niles, Mr. Lorenzen was there to balance those propellers with utmost precision. Even now at the beautiful age of 81, Mr. L. is still propelling. Both he and his exuberant wife, Mary, live in a 135 year old house with memories to spare. I know for a fact that what I saw will one day be displayed in our local St. Joseph Museum. I was told that this quiet and reserved man of the Charles A. Lindbergh era is also a quiet man of God.

A Giant Among Men

"Meet me downstairs in the City Hall", came a clear and articulate voice over the phone. Make no mistake about it, that was Burt Luth talking. This was our first meeting, and I was looking at a man about whom many prolific stories have been written. From what I have heard and read, he surely must have been a giant among men. I was interviewing Niles' retired City Clerk.

I know that a look of amazement clearly was shown on my face, when he said that he once lived in Hancock, Michigan. This little town happens to be a 'stone's throw' from my home. Before we elaborate on this great politician, let's talk first about his birthplace. If you're familiar with the location of Green Bay, Wisconsin, just head toward Lake Michigan in a southerly direction and you will arrive in Manitowoc, which is one of Wisconsin's small seaports. This is Burt Luth's birthplace. The town was predominantly a German settlement and for this reason, the Luths made this their first home. I wonder at this point whether Burt's parents would have changed their final destination, if they had learned more about Door County, which was to become Wisconsin' summer paradise. But Mrs. Luth thought otherwise, when she spotted from the train window the word "Niles" decked out in a floral design. The family stopped here to look around, and this is where they made their final home. This was back in 1907!

Mr. Luth's father was German, and his mother was English. His father's trade was an iron molder, an occupation that he continued with Garden City Fan when moving to Niles. Around 1905, the Luth and Martinson families were inseparable. A person living today just can't imagine how close that date was to the turn of a new century, and now nearing its completion. At any rate, the heads of these families were iron molders and each family moved to different localities whenever a strike ensued. Burt remembered very clearly when his family moved to Hancock, a small town in Upper Peninsula near Portage Lake. Burt recalls the days when he used to watch from Quincy Hill the many scows lighted up at night sailing the Portage Canal. He remembered this one day in particular when the small bridge connecting Houghton and Hancock would not open for an approaching Lake Superior ore freighter, and suddenly saw the ship ram the bridge. "While we lived up here, my father taught me how to hunt and fish, a sport that I continued for many many years." In our interview, he talked about his mother making pasties, which was a dish originated by the English from England, and about the Indians selling them blueberries.

"I remember when I was ten years old and helped my father make cement blocks, which had to be dried then used for building our home. We used a block machine for this job." It was incredible how this 91 year old person presented his story, for it made me feel as though I was with him when he helped his father build their house.

Something that was most outstanding in his memory happened in 1919 when he was twenty years old. He had ten dollars in his pocket and went off to New York where he met his friend, who was a sailor. While his friend's ship was docked at the harbor, the young sailor taught Burt a few tricks about seamanship. Burt was a little apprehensive about that as he had to belong to a union. However, he did go aboard and became an accomplished oiler and water tender of the ship. I believe it was about a month that he sailed the high seas, docking at a few seaports in South America. He remembers in particular being in Buenos Aires, where they handled hundreds of cowhides. It was a great beef country.

The young Mr. Luth graduated from Niles High School in 1917. We didn't elaborate too much about education back then, but it was very obvious that the three R's today were no match with the R's of yesteryear. As I looked over Burt's portfolio, I learned that he was a close friend of Ring Lardner and his family, they were neighbors, as a matter of fact. Burt and Ring played together and often went on buggy and sleigh rides. Mrs. Lardner was known to have invited children over to her house, where they would be treated with cookies and lemonade while she read poetry.

On weekends, Burt used to drive the Express Wagon throughout town loaded with all sorts of vegetables, which were sold at the local grocery stores, one of which was the Bunbury Store. Mr. Luth was a very energetic and versatile person, as he worked in many places doing many different things. His places of employment were the French Paper Company, Kawneer Company, the Metropolitan Life Insurance Company, the Michigan Gas and Electric Company, and finally the Studebaker Assembly Plant.. He told me that in 1941, he was without a job. It was at this time, that one of the local politicians asked him to run for City Clerk, which Burt thought would be an uphill battle to win this position. I guess it was meant to be that Burt Luth was Niles' City Clerk for 32 years. Even today, he looks like an unscathed soldier, and still manages to keep abreast in the political arena. He tells me that he meets with his friends daily at one of the coffee houses. He asked me to join the group when they meet each Tuesday. I was pleased about the invitation, and I thought this would be an excellent time for me to bring along my writing pad. What a story that would be!

Some time ago, a young reader asked me to tell the people about our Broadway Bridge, now known as the Clifford D. Eden Bridge. The reader did emphasize that so many motorists are completely unaware of the name of this structure, much less the life of this person. At this writing, I will give you first hand information about this question. Who would best qualify to give me the answers, if not the person about whom we have written today? When I interviewed Burt in the City's "Oval Office", he had some idea that I would ask him about the man who was responsible for the Broadway Bridge's construction. He had with him, some important data about Niles, about my writings, all of which were scholarly recorded. He handed me the facts about Clifford D. Eden, once our city's engineer. It was through his untiring efforts, skill and knowledge that the bridge in question was designed and eventually constructed. It was truly remarkable how each piece of material matched perfectly, much to the amazement of the bridge's contractor and others who supervised its building. It has been said that Mr. Eden was a quiet, reserved and a dedicated individual, and a gentleman in the truest sense of the word.

To continue with our interview with Burt, he was elated to inform me about his son, Jim, who is an instructor at the Space Center in Florida. Shortly before the Challenger disaster, his son was one of the instructors to be with the astronauts.

Today's meeting with one of our former City Fathers was quite an experience and certainly an honor. In the past, I saw this man so many times and inquired about his identity, and so I was told very emphatically that he was Mr. Burt Luth. So now I left the City Mansion hoping that I would reach that coveted age of 91, being so alert, so spry and intelligent.

Peter Krajci, The Rock

Knowing that eventually I would meet this man, and knowing, too, what kind of a person he was and still is, the title of my Column flashed in my mind. The Ancient Greeks often named their male children, Petros, which meant rock or stone, thus becoming a name of character. In Biblical History, there lived such a person whose name was Peter, and who became a very influential figure. At first, he lacked courage and was weak, but then he became the Rock. Whether our Peter, namely, the one at question, is or was aware of all these qualifications, I do not know. But I do know that he became one of the pillars of this Community.

Without a doubt, Peter Krajci was Niles' pharmaceutical pioneer. He came to the Four Flags City when he was only 12, that was in 1922. He is a Chicagoan by birth, and reared by Slovak parents, who lived in the vicinity of 26th and California Streets. He went to a Catholic school there and was taught by Dominican nuns, who wore the traditional habits. This was their religious garb, which is obviously a far cry from today's dress. Peter tells me that the Sisters liked him, because he did all sorts of errands for these venerable people. The one he remembers well is when he was running all over Chicago trying to find costumes for their school play. He was in seventh grade at the time.

The main reason why his family moved here was because of the "big time robberies" and bootlegging gangs, which were beginning to form. Just the name of Al Capone scared many people. He remembers his cousin who was sort of a lawyer that handled the gang's money. I'm sure that relationship was too close for comfort!

While still in the Windy City, his family belonged to St. Mary's Immaculate Church. It was there that he was baptized. It was in that area that many Slovak immigrants came to this country from Slovakia in the late 1800s and early 1900s. Pete told me the reason why there are so many Slovaks in Niles today. Carl Petruska, Sr., who lived in Chicago at the time, platooned, so to speak, all his closest ethnic friends and made their exit from the big city to Berrien County, where many eventually worked for the railroad.

Right now, I am going to tell you how the Krajci clan came to town. Now this was back in 1922. If you think you have transportation problems, and if you're the one that has been complaining about road construction, and that you're being flagged down too much, then listen to this maneuver. There was a good Samaritan living around here back then named Frank Frucci, Sr., who drove his truck to Chicago to pick up the Krajci family, lock, stock and barrel. It took them 36 to 40 hours riding on rutted gravel roads, sometimes making their own path. Frank's gone now, but the Krajcis live to tell about that beautiful deed. Right then and there, I asked Peter, "If you had your life to live over again, would you have done anything differently?" His answer was quick. "No, sir." Maybe this is why I chose to call him the Rock!

Mr. Krajci is 81 now, and you sure wouldn't think so. He's a 1926 graduate of Niles High School. Just imagine 64 years ago, and to think all the water that went under the bridge! Pete told me that he worked at the Beebe Farm after school for $.25 an hour and also ate there for .$25. He smiled and said, "That was some meal." This young lad must have been a worker, as he also worked for Richter's Pharmacy 215 East Main Street. This was back in 1926 and 1934. There were six drug stores in downtown Niles at the time, namely, Richter's, Dean's, Bidell's, the Royal's and Furguson's. This almost makes you feel as though Mayo's Clinic was nearby.

Peter spent two years at Notre Dame studying to be a pharmacist, a study that he completed in two years. He tells me that he hitchhiked everyday to the University. On this same vein, I would like to quote a letter that Mr. Lee Cousins sent to Pete a month or so ago. It will certainly give us an idea of some business transactions and what it looked like downtown way back then.

"Dear Pete:

While doing some research on the history of Banking in Niles, I ran across the following that I thought might be of interest to you. The northeast corner of Second and Main and has been the site of a historical hotel, prominent Bank and several drug stores. The first recorded occupant of the land was the Union Hotel which was constructed in the 1830s. Records show that the area in front of the Hotel was one big slough, and cattle and wagons repeatedly became mired in the mud. When the city of Niles was incorporated in 1838, the Board of Trustees passed an ordinance requiring the filling up of the pond opposite the Union Hotel on Main Street. For many years following, the corner was the site of the Newman and Snell Bank. Harry Bernard purchased the building in 1924 and opened a drug store. Bernard sold the store to Francis B. Drolet in 1926 who had come from Kalamazoo. Several years later, Drolet sold the store to Ferguson who had been employed by Dean's Drug Store. Pete Krajci, a Niles boy who was the last graduate of the University of Notre Dame pharmacy school before it was discontinued, worked for Ferguson and later bought the store.

With Regards,

Lee Cousins

In 1939, Peter Krajci married Louise Batson, who at one time, taught school here in Niles. This was 1936 and '37. Louise's parents were born in Fiume, Yugoslavia. Today's way would read Rijeka, a famous seaport along the Adriatic Coast. My father would often speak of this location, and would tell me that on a clear day, they could see Italy. You recall that I asked Pete a moment ago whether he would change his style of life, and when I said that, he also said, "that includes my lovely wife, Louise." They have been together for over 50 years!

The Rock continued, "My father worked hard for our growing family. He was making $.25 an hour at Kawneer, and then came home to take care of his big garden, which took care of some necessities. I remember getting a couple of nickels to buy some ice cream or tango bars. We shared a lot, because times were pretty rough."

When a visitor came to town, he often asked, "Where's a good drug store around here?" I am almost certain that his answer would be, "Once you cross St. Joseph's River, you can't miss the building, for on it reads Krajci's." Peter started at this particular spot in 1963 and retired from this professional service in 1969. But in all the years of pharmacy, it was a span of 40 years, 1926-1966.

During our lengthy interview, Pete would often say to me, "none of that flowery stuff, Ed." In all my associations with our senior citizens, I always wish to give credit where credit is due, and believe me, so many of them, all of them, are beautiful people, and what they tell me is like a story book, so richly human.

Before I end my unforgettable chat with Pete, I must tell you of an incident that happened at the Economy Drug Store where Pete once filled out prescriptions for the many happy customers on Niles. As he was busy behind his little counter, he noticed a young man, an ex-con, to be exact, run off with a clock that he had shoplifted. It was just a matter of seconds and Pete took off after him, but he lost him. The police did step in and actually scolded Peter for chasing the thief. They said, "don't you ever do that again, don't you know that he could have shot you!"

Talking with Mr. Krajci was indeed an honor. There's no question that words of wisdom and experience were imparted. Truly an experience that I shall cherish for many years. It is what this elderly man says, how he says it, how he gestures, laughs and smiles, that tells me that he is truly a man of character, and this is why I have called him the Rock. It would take some doing to break this one!

Major William J. Falvey

This is the story about a young high school kid, who became a part of Uncle Sam's Army when he was only a Junior. You see, back then in the late 20s and early 30s, an adolescent could join the CMTC, which was the Citizen Military Training Corps. It could be that this was equivalent to our present ROTC, the Reserve Officers' Training Corps. At any rate, this student was thinking about serving his country.

William J. Falvey was born in Knox, Indiana, where his father worked hard in the clothing business. His father also worked at one time as Time Keeper for the EJE Railroad at Gary, Indiana. Back in 1915, the older Falvey had a General Store, too. He was on the move again, and this is when Ma Falvey stepped in and said, "this is enough moving, besides our son Bill has been in the Second Grade in three different schools!" So Knox it was until 1932. In the meantime, Bill recalls the Yellow river running through this town, the River he used to swim in every day during the summer, fished it and explored it often, and in the winter the kids skated on it. This is when he told me, "my brother and I belonged to a gang called the Northside River Rats." He really laughed when he said that! By the way, Bill is the oldest of seven children, three boys and four girls. While he was in the eighth grade, he remembers being a close friend of Henry Schricker, with whom he often walked to the latter's office. The young student helped to spruce up his place. Some time later this older gentleman became the Governor of Indiana. They say that he always walked about with a white hat, which symbolized a clean government.

He had kind of an embarrassed look on his face when he told me about the day when he carelessly tossed a rock at a passing motorist's windshield. It was just a few moments later when the driver of the car raced over to young Falvey's house and spilled the bad news to his father. It was a whippin' all right, one that he remembered for a long time!

Mr. Falvey was a type of person that befriended many people back in Knox. He talked about a great story Teller by the name of Bunk Seagraves. While I sat there, Bill told me a couple. and right then and there, I had wished that people would be less risqué with their wit, that is other than what Bill told me. He also told me that he met a 102 year old Civil War Veteran from our little town of Pokagon. Do you remember the name of Frank Barton?

During our interview, Bill had all sorts and bits of information that he showed me, and he wanted to make sure that there weren't any unturned stones. He went on to tell that he used to be the carrier for the South Bend Tribune, which was then $.15 a copy, including the Sunday edition. His profit was $.07 per paper.

There was a time in his father's business when things just didn't go right, such as business transactions, partners splitting up, and anything else that may occur in the business world.

I called Bill the night before our meeting, and made plans to drop in the next day. He was waiting for me with a bunch of notes that he had recorded a few hours before my arrival. I must tell you that this man has a memory that can't stop! We talked for a moment, when 'out of the clear blue' he asked, "Well, what do you want to know?" His notes were just topic sentences, and other than that, his speech was memorized! I had enough for a story already. There are indications that his story will be continued.

Mr. Falvey continued, "When I was 14, I used to open my father's store, dusted the counters, and off to school."

Young Bill graduated from high school in 1932, and the Army Reserves, too. He played basketball for the school and later for the city of Knox. Then from 1933 to 1941, he refereed basketball games around town and elsewhere. This is when I asked myself, "what didn't this guy do?" I found out though, that he didn't own a car until he was 30!

He had a happy look on his face when he told me that he was married to Betty Wagner for 53 years. He met her in LaCrosse, Indiana, and he recalls the occasion of their honeymoon, when they drove to Niagara Falls with only $45, and even with some car problems, they came back with some left. We just have to say, "those were the good ol' days." The Falveys were blessed with two sons and two daughters, and at this writing, they all have respectable positions in life, and they gave their parents nine grandchildren and five great grandchildren.'

Let's go back to Knox again and tell you that at one time, the family rented a house for $15 a month. "Egads" and now some of the landlords are asking for astronomical figures for houses where the winds seep through like a sieve! While we're still visiting our friends in this small Indiana town, Bill told me an interesting story about a Chinese midget named Che Mah, who lived a block from the Falvey's residence. Sometimes he used to be pushed in a buggy while he was smoking a cigar! This little man was retired from the Barnum and Bailey Circus, and just wanted to live a normal life. Bill knew him very well. This midget lived to be 88 years old.

Early dates have always fascinated me, and those that I particularly noticed on Mr. Falvey's notes were the years 1915, 1917, 1921, 1922, the 30s and the 40s. Of course, the most important date on record at the moment is 1914, for this is the year when our subject was born, I suppose that the people today would be prone to say, "you came up the hard way, didn't you?" You bet he did, just take a look at the results and we we're not finished yet!

In 1935 twenty-one year old William graduated from the Army Reserves as Second Lieutenant. He trained at different Camps during the summer months, places such as Camp Wolters, Texas, Camp Barkley, Texas, then the Louisiana Maneuvers, the California Desert, Fort Dix, N.J. and finally at Birmingham, England. He had a feeling that war clouds were shaping up and he'd often check his uniform in the family closet. On the day of the Pearl Harbor Attack, he remembers very vividly listening to the Green Bay Packers and Chicago Bears. There was a Special Delivery the very next day, December 8, telling this Second Lieutenant to report for duty. When W.W.II broke out, the young Army Officer predicted that it was going to last four years, and his predictions were very close.

I didn't wish to question Mr. Falvey too closely about war matters, as I thought that he may have resented it. On the contrary, he knew that I was curious, so he continued with his deliberate and soft spoken way. He did emphasize that the U.S. Army took a beating on D-Day. In early 1944, his outfit sailed to England, where they belonged to the Regimental S-2. "Security was tight," he said, "I had charge of all the maps." He went on to tell me that they slept in secret rooms, for fear of someone talking in his sleep and thus revealing the invasion plans. This was known some 90 days in advance.

Somebody told me, "Did you know that Bill Falvey was a Major in the Army?" Here was my chance to find out face to face. You talk about a modest man, when he told me the truth about this promotion. Now I was really curious and asked him, "Where did all these promotions take place?" "My Second Lieutenant rating came in the California desert in 1943, and on July 6, 1944, after being in France 30 days or so, they made me Major while being on the battlefield," he proudly smiled. I could have sat by his side for hours listening to some real stuff. No doubt the Major still misses his buddies, the Privates, the Corporals, the Sergeants and even the Colonels that fell in battle. He recalls the time that he was sent together with a Doctor and Interrogator to investigate a concentration camp at Fassenberg, Germany. At the time, there were 15,000 prisoners living at the Camp, and he told me that within the last five years, there were 75,000 that already had died. Today, Mr. Falvey has a book, in the German language, that was authored by one of the inmates of that Camp. I am sure that the retired Major has many writings and autographs of other Army Personnel. I just had to ask him, "Did you ever meet General Patton?" "Oh yes, several times," was his quick answer. I was almost tempted to ask him if he ever heard the General use profanity? He no doubt would have said something like, "does a duck swim?"

Going back again to his early school days, he still can't understand how a 14 year old kid would walk with a man that was 40-50 years old almost daily. It could be that this is why today this man has so many friends. He walked back then, and you can still see him walking about today!

Do you remember when we told you in our segment of the story about young William being in the Second Grade in three different schools? No wonder his mother was so concerned, as the father was continuously moving, first it was Knox, then Winimac, Gary, Buffalo, Ossanin and LaPorte. I guess he wanted to prove that he was a true Hoosier.

The Falvey clan owned several stores, twelve located in Indiana, and two in Michigan. Mr. Falvey started the store in Niles in 1946, and from that time until the early 80s, he traveled quite extensively for his line of business. Whenever he did go, he would always ask some other store owner or two to accompany him on these trips. At this time, I would like to tell you about these lucky people, namely, Fred Reynolds from the Hardware Store, Charles Basso, the Tavern Keeper, William Skalla, the rural route mailman, W.F. Harrah, the owner of National Standard, the ever talked-about Walter Zable, the Principal of Niles High School, LeRoy Heberley, a

Salesman, Jack Kennedy, owner of the Meat Company, John Tinan, the Grocer, and O.S. Duff, owner of a Printing Press, and active member of the City Council, even at the age of 90, and it was through his maneuvering that the present structure of the Library was developed.

Mr. Falvey still remembers some of the first people that came to his store in '46, one was Ed O'Brien who bought a Kromer Railroad cap, the other was Fred Foster, who bought some Wolverine Shoes, and then Marshall Grathwohl, who bought a pair of Florsheim Shoes. "Funny thing about those shoes I sold him, one shoe was size seven and the other was size eight!", Bill laughed. "What a way to start a business!"

I really had no intention of ending my story about this soldier, but the Press people allow me just so many lines. So, in my closing thoughts, may I say that he is somebody special. I know there are others like he in our midst, but I was just lucky enough to have rung his door bell. As I was leaving, he commented about how wonderful his wife was during their many years of wedded life. He's grateful to the many people who helped them. Niles indeed is fortunate to have a man blessed with experience, wisdom and staunch faith.

Major Bill Falvey and I sat tête-à-tête in one of the upper flats of downtown the other day, and we talked about his recent European trip. You see, this excursion to the Old World was on Bill's mind for quite some time. He has had a plan, together with many other W.W.II Veterans, that on June 4, 1994, they will commemorate the 50th anniversary of the Normandy Invasion.

I had wished that everyone would really get to know Mr. Falvey. You don't have to wonder why he was chosen to be a Major, for the Army was his way of life for many years. He enjoys talking about the past, for it makes him feel that you cared about what took place 50 years ago. Bill was an Intelligence Officer of the 90th Division, which was known as the "tough hombres". "It was a terrible day", the Major said. I could almost see some tears, as he lost many dear friends. He certainly has very unpleasant memories of that fateful day on the beaches of Normandy. The most beautiful memory, however, was the smell of victory for his men, for the U.S. Army, and indeed for all the people of America.

Besides this man's gentle attitude, he had another attribute that was noticeable. He was humble. During our visit, he went to his suitcase, which was loaded with memorabilia from W.W.II. This was information that he had gathered on his recent flight. The top of the list, of course, was his 90th Infantry Division. He was proud of his men, and he would often say to me, "We sure had a bunch of tough hombres."

Major Falvey gave me some other detailed information about that awful day in France and the aftermath. He recalls the many months that his troops and the civilians had to walk in total darkness in fear of being detected by the enemy.

The Major's trip to Europe was fruitful, indeed, as he and other dignitaries were making definite plans for the forthcoming gala affair. Since the War's end, he has been in touch with many French people, particularly those who were the leaders of the underground. There came a moment in the heat of battle that a certain German Commander gave a four hour truce to the Americans, who were in Major Falvey's Division, so that they could pick up their fallen comrades. And since that memorable day on Normandy soil, the Major has kept in touch with this fighting humanitarian.

There is one person in particular that Bill Falvey corresponds with in France today, and that is Henri Levaufre, whom he befriended in 1971, and since that moment the bond of friendship still exists. It was in 1971 that these two men formally met, and since that moment the bond of friendship still exists.

Undoubtedly, another unforgettable moment in the Major's wartime maneuvers was the liberation of the prisoners at the Flossenberg Concentration Camp, located on the Czech and German border.

While he was in Belgium, he talked to many former inmates of the Camp. He also met with a French contingent and other Belgians to arrange a joint ceremony at Bostagne, Belgium.

Major Falvey of the 90th Infantry Division has been working with many other U.S. Army Personnel to attend the Normandy event. On this Anniversary, there will be 50 buses, the itinerary extending from England to France, then to Luxemburg and Belgium, and finally to Germany. You might have guessed that one of the narrators of these buses will be none other than Major William Falvey from Niles, Michigan. This journey to all these countries will be called the Battle Route Tour.

Those with whom he has been in contact from this general area are as follows: Don Thompson from Osceola; Robert Morman from Mishawaka; Joseph Kujanik from Gary; Clifton Flora from Cedar Lake; Paul Beck from Goshen; Robert Ranschaert, Joseph Przestor, Verne Kryder, Louis Kolozsor and Kenneth Felger all from South Bend.

All types of Military Units will participate in this tour, which will include the Infantry, the Paratroopers, Glider Units, Tank Divisions, Fighter Pilots, Bomber Pilots, Navy Outfits and Recon Troops.

Mr. Falvey handed me his European itinerary, which I would like to synopsize for you. On March 24 of this year, they left by Jet Liner from Chicago to London. They rested a bit on the 25th because of the Jet Lag, though the remainder of the day was spent at Tower Hotel, concluding with dinner at London's famous Beefeater. On the 26th, they were guests of the British Paratroopers and also visited a W.W.II American Airbase. Perhaps one of the most satisfying points of the journey was their visit to historic Normandy. This was done on Friday, March 27. They stopped at the Omaha Beach Cemetery on March 28, where 650 of Major Falvey's "tough hombres" were buried. They also made it their business to coordinate the plans with other divisions, who are currently making arrangements for the anniversary. On Sunday the 29th, they saw the Battle of Normandy Museum. On the 30th of March, their tour took them to Reims, the site of the German capitulation on May 8, 1945. At Verdun, they saw the gravesite of 130,000 unknown French soldiers of W.W.I. Later that day, they stopped to see General Patton's burial ground at Luxemburg.

On Tuesday, March 31, the Major and his friends viewed the W.W.II Museum in Diekirch, and cruised the Bostagne area. They spent several hours at Brussels, where they met with the former inmates of the Flossenburg Camp. This same group hopes to meet at Bostagne in June 1994. Their visit, at this point, continued on to April 1. Ever since the Major's arrival, there was much talk about the 50th Anniversary. It was truly a special occasion for him to be with some of the inmates again, especially the first prisoner he met back in 1945. Because he cared so much for these people, he was awarded two medals from the Belgium Government during his recent trip.

On April 2, they left Brussels for the Airport, where a 747 was waiting for their return trip to America. His office here in Niles has been busy ever since his return, writing letters and notes to people throughout the U.S., reminding them about the great event, even though there is much time remaining. I can tell you one thing, this man has already started the countdown for D-Day's Anniversary.

It would interest our readers to note that this man of war has returned to the ol' sod on ten different occasions. It could be to renew old acquaintances, or to strengthen his many bonds of friendship. Being the warm person that he is, he visited the grave sites of many of his men, those "tough hombres". He would always leave these quiet places by saying Requiescant in Pace.

The people of Niles and vicinity are hoping that this great historic day will come to pass, and that still a trace of that 90th Infantry Division will be glad to have their Major Bill Falvey by its side.

So, to him and his spouse, we say Bon Voyage!

The Jack Stanner Story

This is the story that I've been trying to corral for weeks, and finally he showed up at the front door. There was no mistake about it, it was Jack Stanner sporting his large gray mustache. I believe it's the only one of its kind in Niles, I think he knows it, and that's why he's proud to own it. Jack is 73 now and there is a certain style about this man that you must admire. There's no question in my mind that he resembles a general of the Civil War era. This is the gentleman that I told you about that had a great grandmother who was a spy during Lincoln's time. In a way, I am kind of putting things together today, namely, his relative running back and forth to different camps, and now her grandson looking like a typical war hero with mustache and all. Kind of a pleasant memory, isn't it?

I must admit that there's something about this person that baffles me at the moment. It could be that I may have seen a character on some TV miniseries. At any rate, it was his boyish smile and rasping chuckle that moved me. He brought with him a couple of sheets of information for which he would have almost sacrificed his life. One sheet showed off Eliza Fields, Jack's great grandmother, the Civil War sweetheart. That certain look on her face almost told you something, like a face of utter determination. As I am writing this, I have that photo before me and it tells me a story about a lot of things. Jack's father is also in the picture, a nice looking man, I might add. I keep looking at Eliza and I see the resemblance of some Indian blood. I say this, as I lived among the Indians in Upper Michigan, and they have those distinct features. The photo is about eighty year old and I wish I had a direct line of communication with every subject standing and sitting there. The other sheet was a copy of a publication printed years ago during Eliza's birthday, 94th to be exact. The print of which is not too clear so please bear with me and I will give it as I see it. The article reads as follows:

"Years have failed to dim Mrs. Eliza Fields' recollection of a bit of verse that brought her and Simeon Fields into marriage more than three score years ago. Mrs. Fields was then a nurse for the confederate forces and her sweetheart was a soldier in the Union Army. On her ninety-fourth birthday, Friday, Mrs. Fields recited the "courtin days" poetry for her guests. At the close of the War, "Nurse Eliza" and the author were married. Civil War experiences ride high in the memory of Mrs. Fields. She recalls one incident during the war when the Union Forces took a horse from her home. Her sister told of the horse being taken. Immediately, Mrs. Fields mounted another horse and gave chase overtaking the forces several miles from her home. She found her horse and reported the matter to the commanding officer. He compelled the rider to return the mount. Mrs. Fields also recalls the time when she ran a steamboat on the Mississippi River. The name of the boat was the Fair. During the war when on a visit to Little Rock, Arkansas, she was compelled to swear allegiance to the Union before she could return to her home. She still has the certificate of allegiance and cherishes it with the memory of her childhood days. During recent years, Mrs. Fields has been gradually failing in health. Now she is hardly able to get around the house. Her living relatives are her son, John Fields, Pocatello, Idaho; a grandson, Albert Stanner, Niles, Michigan; granddaughters, Marie Fields, Chicago, Illinois; and Mrs. Marie Mullane, Panama Canal Zone; and six grandchildren. Relatives in Council Bluffs are Mrs. W.C. Burke; and Miss Charlotte Woodward; nieces; and Ray Fields a nephew. Among her birthday guests were Rev. Dr. A.A.

Heath, pastor of Broadway Methodist Church, and Episcopal Church, which Mrs. Fields has attended for many years. Rev. Dr. Ralph W. Livers, St. John's English Lutheran Church, Rev R.R. Brown, Christian and Missionary Alliance Church, Omaha. Mrs. Fields lives with Mr. and Mrs. Langfelt on Grand Avenue.

Now that was a courageous young lady to be scouting around from North to South and back again, dodging bullets and possibly facing execution for her adventurous deed! Is there a slim chance of finding someone in these parts to start a novel using Eliza Fields as the principal character?

During our visit, Jack told me about an incident that made his eyes look like two saucers! This was back in the '20s when he was just a kid as he was walking west on the 500 block of Broadway Street, which was gravel then, when all of a sudden, here comes a motorcycle cop by the name of Carl Volker going hell bent for election chasing and shooting at either a professional bank robber or bootlegger. Jack just couldn't believe what he was watching. This incident brings to mind the many times that our local policemen are chasing either speeding cars or motorcycles through our alleys, fields and people's yards! Those of you who read this and have seen this, know quite well what I'm talking about.

Mr. Stanner tells me he's been living around here for 70 years or so. Geez, that's close to three quarters of a century and some people have the audacity to say that old folks don't know too much. Try them sometime. All I can say is that there's been a lot of turbulent waters that went under the bridge!

This happy mustached person also said that while he was in the U.S. Army stationed at Hawaii, his great grandmother sent him three dollars as a legacy. That was back in the '40s and that amount meant something. He would recall back in the '20s again when the farmers came to town with their horse drawn wagons filled with garden produce ringing a bell telling the neighborhood about their arrival. He also remembers Chet Curtis plowing snow with his homemade plow pulled by a horse. Jack just kept on telling me things with that certain grin on his face. He said his wife hates gravy today because she had so much of that flour gravy during the Depression. Another popular food then was popcorn. He also told about the diaper pail, which today would almost be scorned. Back then when a diaper was used to its fullest purpose, it was then used as a cleaning rag. This was during the Great Depression when people were squeezing nickels and dimes.

His father owned an electrical store, he continues, and this one day his father said, "Son, would you go over to this one person and collect whatever he owes me," and Jack, being that gentle a person, answered, "Dad, I just can't do that." Maybe people think that was being very disrespectful, but on the contrary, in the good ol' days, we didn't know how to spell that word!

During that time when a person got a job, it was like taking the bull by the horns. His first big paycheck was fifty-five dollars.

In the course of our conversation, I asked him where his wife was from. He said, "Tustin, Michigan." Any city headed north always interested me. This is near Cadillac some four hours from here.

He mentioned a Studebaker wagon, which would park along Dowagiac Creek near Schmidt's Packing Company catching sturgeon fish. I do know that a sturgeon can get as long as six feet, and I can't picture all those fish in a wagon!

In closing, here was a man that every time he said something, he had a smile on his face and a chuckle that only belonged to Jack Stanner.

Seventy Years of Wedded Bliss

Some weeks ago, the nice people of Brandywine AARP invited my spouse and me to a potluck luncheon at the Pepper Martin Park. They asked me to tell them some stories about the U.P. You might have known that I was in my glory! About the only thing I didn't tell them was where all the good fishin' holes were. I asked my audience how many had ever visited this Superior Land. There were several that did and just then the lady sitting to my right whispered to me about an elderly couple in the crowd who had recently celebrated their 70th Wedding Anniversary. It was just a few weeks after that that I had the honor to interview these wonderful people. By the way, those people from Brandywine sure put on a good spread!

What a memorable occasion that must have been to celebrate seventy years of wedded life! Sixty-five of these commendable years were spent under the same roof. May all of us take great pride in congratulating Mr. and Mrs. Russ Grafford. What a noticeable transition from July 6, 1921 to July 6, 1991!

On May 14, 1990, the tiny town of Byron, Indiana hailed the birth of a boy who was to be called Russell. The town of Byron just isn't on the map anymore, but its son is, and believe me he remembers many many things. During my visit in his home, I was absolutely amazed to learn the number of dates of special events that he knew in a lifetime and the numbers that he has memorized such as his and his spouse's Social Security, Policies and many other important data. I didn't wish to insult him as to whether he used some kind of computer. His faculties were positively superb. I compared them to some of our present day "book worms". You could tell that he was geared to tell me a lot of things. His lovely lady just sat and listened. Her turn was coming.

Russ said that in 1907 he had an armless teacher, whose penmanship was incredibly beautiful. He remembers the year 1908 when someone had started the spiritual revolution stating that the end of the world will come at high noon on this particular day. He used to see his grandparents watching the clock to strike at noon. This they did very religiously for many days.

Russ left the room for a moment and came back with a photo picturing him with his prized billy goat harnessed to a coaster wagon. "This was my transportation back then", he smiled.

He remembered the sinking of the Titanic.

While I am recording all these remarkable dates, I didn't realize that I was telling you things that were almost the beginning of the 20th Century and here it is close to the 21st! What those who lived back then did to pave the way for our smooth sailing we find ourselves now on turbulent waters.

Mr. Grafford worked for the Kawneer Company for forty years and during that time, he also engineered the building of his present house. He was responsible for 99% of the work. If we lived in 1926, we would have seen him pushing his wheelbarrow full of dirt which was used for landscaping his yard. He used the pick and shovel to dig his basement and this was the dirt that he hauled.

He led me to his kitchen and showed me their round table which they had since the knot was tied and, frankly, it outmatched some of our modern stuff. While I was in this eating place, Russ showed me some of the trim around the wainscotting especially his way of hiding the nail heads. Really, if one would listen carefully to all that he tells you, you could go home with some nifty plans.

As the years went by, he told me that he kept a file of all the car designs and their cost.

"My first well," he said, "was dug by myself." He continued, "My present water supply is taken care of by professional people." With all the digging, including the basement, the building of the house, the landscaping and directing traffic at the Kawneer Plant, you might say that Russ was a determined individual. You might also say that this is why he lived to enjoy seventy years of married life.

Now, Dagney, the tall stately lady of the house is the daughter of immigrant parents from Oslo, Norway. Her family first moved to the Copper Country where her father worked for the Copper Range Railroad. Her uncle was first to land in the New World, and then followed by the other members of this Norwegian family. In 1916, her parents moved to Niles and this is when the father continued his work with the Michigan Central. Oh, yes, she pointed out the kitchen window and showed me where the street car used to run all the way from South Bend to St. Joseph. Naturally, we got on the subject of our youth of today and she sighed, "Oh, my." We didn't go on anymore, as it wasn't good. These people should know, they've been around.

The Graffords have been world travelers, have seen all the States and their Capitals, plus a few other countries. They enjoyed their annual Florida visits for several years and this is where Russ became a camera buff. I am beginning to think that Russ' hobby is his annual Christmas display, which, by the way, was all invented by Mr. Grafford. He showed me pictures of this life-sized "city of animals and people." He said that it takes him about a month to put up this Christmas exhibition.

There are eleven great grand children in the Grafford lineage, and Russ provides them with all kinds of play things. The grandmother and great grandmother told me, "My daughter-in-law is like a daughter to me." It was quite obvious to know why.

Martin Daly

This 83 year old man told me that his family worked very hard back in the early 1900s in the Sister Lakes area. Martin Daly's father came from Ireland and his mother was born in the little settlement of Riverside near the thriving city of Benton Harbor. I believe the older Daly must have smelled the blossoms of this Fruit Land before his boat harbored in New York.

Before I moved to these parts, I never dreamed that this was the land of abundant fruit. The natives of Upper Michigan never spoke of this blossomland and it was not until today's interview that I first learned more about these rich fruit farmlands. Had you asked me what grew in the north country, I would have told you that Copper was the biggest harvest found in the belly of the earth.

It must have been extremely hard to work with several horses, instead of high powered tractors. Now we're talking about way back in the 1890s when spraying first came to be. Martin went back to his childhood when he emphasized that they never asked "why" when told to do something. It was done! It's a different story today with all the compromises.

Back on their Round Lake farm, they had a few milking cows which were milked in the morning by his father and in the evening by him and his brothers. Besides all this, they had six working horses to care for. He remembers his mother making quite a bit of butter and I imagine everyone had a hand with the churning.

Most kids walked to school, others perhaps transported by wagon or sled. Martin told me that a snow storm never stopped them from going to school. Their one-room school house took care of 30-40 students from grades 1-8. The teacher not only taught, but was the janitor, custodian and tender of cuts and bruises. At the beginning of each day, some older boy had the chore of bringing in a pail of drinking water. Each subject was taught about ten minutes to all of the eight grades.

This elderly man told me about an incident that happened in 1919 while they were picking strawberries out in the field. A sudden lightening storm came up and they all tore to a shed that was nearby. It seems that taking shelter in this shed was the wrong place to be, as lightening did strike this small building. Two of the boys were hit by the bolt, one, whose shoe was completely ripped off his foot. They say that some of the shoes back then had some metal part, hence the reason why the bolt struck that part. The other boy was burned around his waist, as the belt that he wore had a metal buckle.

As a youngster, Martin remembers hitching a ride on the Big Mac truck carrying fruit to Benton Harbor's landing dock. This is where the freighters with fruit and produce were loaded and shipped to Chicago. I would like to think that I was somewhere on that dock, watching, listening and talking and perhaps asking one of the seamen about his journeys across Lake Michigan.

Since Martin's parents were some of the early pioneers of fruit farming, he continued to tell me about the acreage of strawberries, dewberries, apples, including some "dutchies", peaches, sweet cherries and pears.

The parish that he attended as a youngster was called the Sacred Heart Mission, administered by the clergy at Dowagiac. The Mission today and its adjacent cemetery gives evidence of the many settlers that worked in that area in the early 1900s. This was Indian Country, too, and as Martin puts it, "the Indians always used the last four pews of the church." At that time, the parishes were administered by the Basilian

Fathers. It was through their influences and encouragement of his parents, that young Martin entered a private school at Windsor, Ontario, Canada. This was in 1926-27, the year the Ambassador Bridge was built connecting the United States and Canada. I was rather curious to know more about this young scholastic's Order of the Day while he was in school. Believe me, it is indeed a far cry from today's schedule. He did give me a few specifics, such as rising at 6:00 a.m., attending church services dressed in coat and tie, breakfast at 7, study hall from 8-9, with classes from 9-12, and then again in the afternoon. Here are just a few of his academic achievements, namely, Latin, French, English, Physics, Chemistry, Algebra, Geometry and Christian Doctrine. Besides this heavy schedule, I pictured him being a football star. He knew that I taught Latin, so with a big grin, he conjugated a Latin verb which he learned 65 years ago! Because of ill health, Martin was unable to further his studies.

Frankly, I wish that most of our affluent students would be exposed to this academic challenge. In all probability, our society wouldn't be as heavily plagued with scars as it is today.

The Tennessean

I met a man from Coffee County, Tennessee the other day and it didn't take too long to find out that he was a very kind, gentle and caring person.

He knew I was coming and he was ready to tell me about himself, about some of the places and other Tennesseans. He told me that he was born in Beechgrove, a tiny village cozily nestled among the hills and plateaus of Tennessee. Once he started talking, there was no way that I could have stopped him, for he was so full of enthusiasm.

This was his time to reminisce, and believe me, his story was exciting and thorough. If only those with whom he had associated as a youngster would have been here to hear him! I'm sure that they, too, would have told their part about life in Coffee County.

He was that type of a person that could have had an audience that would have listened to him for hours.

People from the deep South have always fascinated me and this gentleman from Beechgrove was no exception. If I were to calculate the mileage between my birthplace and his it would be in the neighborhood of 1,200 miles. Now you are able to note the different dialects between the North and the South.

Because I was charmed and captivated by his way of expression, I listened carefully and attentively to every piece of information that I could muster. He didn't wish to be in any limelight, so he asked me that his identity remain anonymous. His family back home was poor like so many others in that region. This dates back to the middle 20s. He told me that all the roads were gravel, and if you wanted to get anywhere, you would either walk or take one of the farm mules. Since he lived on a farm, there really wasn't much time to go anywhere other than work the fields of corn and hay and tending the cows and hogs. Mules were more often used than horses, as they were sturdier and more efficient with hillside plows.

His father once owned a general store which made his work on the farm more demanding. At night, they burned kerosene lamps, as they did in so many other places in the 20s. Outhouses or privies were common real estate. When he became of school age, he remembers coming home from school, sitting down to eat, and then taking off for the fields.

"We never worked on Sundays," he said, and "when Monday came around, back to my chores."

"We always carried pocket knives, which we used for whittling," he continued. He showed me a tiny pair of pliers and fence post diggers that he had whittled out of soft pine wood.

"I remember taking care of the teacher's horse. Our teacher was very strict, and I do mean strict. There was always a long switch hanging in this one room school house, and he used it, too," he exclaimed. Since there was no running water in the school, they took turns fetching a bucket of water from the nearby spring. He recalls crawling underneath a barbed wire fence to get to the well.

The boys often used slingshots to kill small wild game for meat on the table. He told me about this one long cave that looked like a long room where they would roast hot dogs over a fire. While they ate, they listened for water drops coming from the cave's ceiling falling into the well with that certain sound.

He remembers this one man coming to his area with a team of mules pulling a covered wagon selling groceries. All these goodies were neatly shelved in the wagon. Today he misses this man, for some years ago he was on his way to visit him and was killed in a car accident.

"I remember during the cold winter nights, we used to heat the flat irons and wrap them up and put them in the bed to keep us warm," he smiled. He continued, "If I wasn't sawing wood, I'd be cutting it and piling it. And if I wasn't doing that, then I'd be in the pigpen feeding the porkers, or I'd be feeding the chickens, watering the livestock or bailing hay or picking corn by hand. You might say that I worked hard."

I asked him what he did for recreation.

"We'd be pickin' music and we'd walk for miles to pick with guitars, fiddles, banjos and mandolins. We played softball, basketball and pitched horseshoes. We played hard. It sure was nice to get away from all that work."

He went on to say, "I must tell you about a feud that happened at one of our school box socials. There was a fatal stabbing this one day and it was real bad. People down there do a lot of fightin' and feudin' and there were many times that they would drink real bad!"

All this while I just looked, listened and laughed as it was all said with that Southern flavor. The part that I enjoyed the most was when I asked him, "Did people have stills?"

He was quick to say, "Oh, yeah." Then he began to tell me about how he knew who would have them. Anytime they noticed some white smoke over the horizon, they would say, "there goes one."

I said, "I'm sure the Feds used to chase all the violators," and he came back with, "Oh, yeah, you bet." We were almost finished talking about these "illegal spirits" when he told me about one day when some friends of his invited him over to their place to watch how a still works. He told me, "The one I saw was really a beauty with all that coiled copper tubing, and besides this one was located right next to a running stream, which was perfect!" He also told me about

62

some people having moonshine that was about 140 proof! So goes the distilling world!

This hard working man told me about Uncle Pete Urp, no relation to him nor to too many other people, but this is what he said, "He was a very, very kind man and he would do most anything for anyone, but he drank bad! He used to invite us kids to come over and use his .22 rifle and shoot at targets in the backyard. There were many times when we would go by his house and we'd see him on his chair leaning against the porch or whittling on some piece of wood making something to give away. He really was a good man. He had that one weakness." The name Uncle Pete Urp came up so many times, that I know he was truly an exceptional person.

Our man from Coffee County left me with some beautiful enduring thoughts that he wanted me to share with today's youth. Tell them to be, "God fearing, work hard, don't take anything that doesn't belong to you, mind your own business, and above all, be honest."

I was firmly convinced that what he said he, himself, carried out to the letter. These were his cardinal rules, no matter what.

The Arkansans

Last week, we traveled the hills and plateaus of Tennessee and visited a man of country music. Today, we'll visit with Mr. and Mrs. L.D. Carter from Woodruff County, Arkansas, 83 and 79 years young respectively. I had the good fortune of meeting this elderly gent at the Eastgate Shopping Center some weeks ago. We talked about the weather, his garden and about world affairs in general. He impressed me with his Southern drawl. Here was another chance for me to tell my readers about another person from the South. I told him that I had a weekly Column in our local newspaper about people living "back then". I asked him, "would you like to have me stop by and interview you?" He didn't hesitate a moment to say, "Why not?"

I called him today and said that I would be over this morning. He knew who I was immediately and said, "Come on, the coffee's good and hot." I liked the way he said that!

He and his wife LouVenia were so pleased to have me sit by them and talk about old times. It was just a matter of minutes when they told me that they were married 63 years. What a remarkable bond! I thought of this in comparison to today's knots and it looks like we have a lot of catching up to do. Usually when one visits another's house, your eyes capture something outstanding. I couldn't help but notice on the dining room table a large Holy Bible which gave me some indication why they had such a prolonged life together.

Yes, the coffee was good and hot. LouVenia saw to that. L.D. Started in, "I remember when." This was repetitious throughout our conversation. Mr. Carter was born in Limestone County, Alabama and moved to McCrory,

Arkansas as a teenager. They were farmers and they worked hard raising row crops as corn, cotton and beans. They had horses and mules until the arrival of the farm tractor around 1945.

L.D. told me that there was a time when the family bought 80 acres of land much of which was timber. The top price was $300 but he did profit by selling the timber once it was cut. This was free range country where the cattle and hogs roamed about. The cattle were all branded and the hogs were also marked. They raised much rice on their land. While they were building their house in 1920, he helped dig a 40 foot well. In their house, they had a kerosene lamp and their toilet facility was, of course, like many people in America, the well known privy. He told me about their winters having little snow but still very chilling temperatures.

He took great pride when he told me how he met his bride of 63 years. She being a farmer also, was milking the cows when L.D. came by. When he said this, she stood by with a very satisfied and grateful look.

He told me that he walked to school which was a half mile or so from the Ol' homestead. He looked quite modest when LouVenia said that he played the harmonica at the local dances. Some time in 1918, I guess it was, when a bi-plane buzzed around town and landed in a nearby field. The whole town came out to see this spectacle! When he was a kid, he owned a bicycle and in 1920, he drove a car for the first time. One of his jobs, he says, was driving a taxi in McCrory.

After his taxi stint, L.D. worked in a bottling factory. He tells me that 1937 during the Mississippi River's overflow, it was one of the worst floods they had which forced them to build a sort of platform to protect their hogs. In 1945, he became a surveyor working primarily in Woodruff County. Both he and LouVenia talked about a Diamond Mine that was once in operation in that area but now there is just a pit where you'll find people digging the surface looking for that precious gem. Not too far from their land there were rich produce farms and peach groves.

"In the foothills of the Ozarks," he says, "Many farmers raised chickens and turkeys and there were many eggs on the market. I remember getting together with the local folks at their special barbecues listening to County Candidates running for Office. During those days, the boys and young men would play a lot of baseball and horseshoes and many folks would do a lot of square dancin'. When I wasn't doing any farm chores, I'd be huntin' squirrels, rabbits and coons."

During my visit with the Carters, there were moments when I was left alone in the living room. I knew why they both disappeared. They were looking for something to show me. L.D. came out of the kitchen first and said to me, "Did you ever see an okra this long before? It came from my garden." It was over three feet long and it looked like a small missile! He had a grin on his face that was almost as long! Here came LouVenia out of their bedroom with stacks of picture albums and loose photos of the whole clan. That was a story in itself. They had every right to be proud of their four sons plus all the grand and great-grand-children, cousins and what all. I marveled at the way that she was shuffling those pictures, as I knew there were some in that bunch that needed some tall explainin'. I wonder how many people in this community have the distinction of being blissfully married for 63 years. And of course, with those many years also come many pictures, albums, photos, portraits, clippings, newspapers, momentos, souvenirs and gifts. you might have known that L.D. came along with some of his prized photos. But the greatest "show and tell" of the day was LouVenia's genealogy which started in 1830 and is arranged to the present day. If you were to ask what the dimension of this notebook was, I would have to tell you that it is at least three inches thick. She was so elated to show me a picture of her great-grand father, James Alfred Adcock, and also his tomb on which an inscription read, "Born October 9, 1830, Died April 25, 1914. Buried at Crossroads Cemetery in Arkansas. C.O.D. 14th Kansas Infantry (Union)."

I've been fixin' to tell you that back in 1926 when good ol' L.D. was working for a Delco Light plant as its mechanic, his buddies used to call him Delco. It was brought to my attention by LouVenia that her grandson, Captain John Quick, used to pilot the helicopter on which President and Mrs. Reagan were passengers on short excursion trips within the Capitol.

The Carter family undoubtedly reaches out to many parts of our country as the family tree indicates. The faces of these people portray a sense of deep pride, faith and patriotism. It is obvious that they have so much to talk about and being that there are many numbers in this clan, it is truly an open book! I am sure that the Carter family has had a reunion or at least has thought of one or is currently planning for one. This is one get-together I would like to see!

The home of these two Arkansans was indeed warm and congenial. It was nothing flashy or gaudy, but pure, simple and rich with loving memories. With a lineage as elaborate as theirs, what else can they say, but, "We remember when."

You no doubt have noted that I enjoy talking about the past, what people did for a living, how big of a family they had, their home life, school days, going to church on Sundays, and what was their social life. The years in the 20th Century are running short, and I want to tell all that there is, before the next one comes around and the way I see it now, the happy days are also growing short.

Ivanka

Some weeks ago, I told you that I'd be interviewing someone from Yugoslavia. Well, that certain someone is Ivanka Ritter, nee Golovic, born in Metlika, Slovenia, Yugoslavia. When foreign names are pronounced properly, it is like a beautiful sound of a musical instrument. Ivanka heard about my stories and she called me one day and said that she would like to tell me about her life in Europe and America. She did just that. Her English was "broken" but I must tell you that it was unmistakably most pleasing.

Before I go on to tell you about this intelligent immigrant, I must first tell you something about Yugoslavia, which, by the way, is also the birthplace of my parents. This scenic country is divided into regions or republics, namely, Slovenia, Croatia, Bosnia, Hercegovina, Macedonia, Montenegro, and Serbia. Incidentally, do you remember Sarajevo, Serbia, the Home of the Winter Olympics some years ago? Should one be encountered on the street and asked, "What nationality are you?" and he answers, "I am a Yugoslav," his response at this point would be incorrect. One should be more specific and state that he is a Slovene, from Slovenia, Yugoslavia, or I am a Croat from Croatia, Yugoslavia and so on.

Much of today's populace is unaware of Yugoslavia's republics. It has often happened that people have asked about my ethnic background and I tell them that I am a Croat and they will inevitably ask me, "What's that?" This is when my Slavic blood takes another course! The different regions of this country does make it difficult for many to remember all the various languages. But when you wonder why is it that most Europeans know our geological locations quite well, not only that, but in addition many of whom speak English flawlessly, though with a foreign accent.

Knowing that both of us were more or less of the same bloodline that is, of Slavic origin, Ivanka now began her story in earnest in her quaint English way and also in Slovenian and Croatian which I also understood. This even helped me to brush up on my native tongue which I have not used for many years, for this was the language I spoke when I was a child. She started to show me maps and all kinds of foreign literature. I brought along a map of Yugoslavia, a map that I had in my possession for years, as there was a time I used to correspond with my relatives in that country. I was curious to know exactly where they lived. Would you know that Ivanka also had a better map? For this nice lady, it was "back home again." It was a glorious meeting for both of us.

As a ten-year-old girl living in Metlika, she helped her father cook for thirty workers on his big vineyard. Her mother had pneumonia then and was too weak to do any work so it was her job to take care of the farmlands. She remembers cooking big meals for breakfast, lunch and supper and for dessert, she made many, many donuts.

When she became older, they moved to Ljublanja, a city of 350,000 people. She finally decided to visit her sister in Chicago and someone drove her to Rijeka, one of Yugoslavia's great seaports. It was there that she boarded a ship to New York. This ship carried freight and passengers and this was its maiden voyage. While they were abroad, the captain was asked to divert the ship to another port in America because of some maritime difficulty. So they landed at Newport News, Virginia on July 26, 1960. She went to Chicago by rail and met her sister who was 26 years her senior. After a while, she pleaded with her sister to find her a job where she could earn a few dollars. This is when she was emphatically ignored and this is when Ivanka started to cry.

Her name, incidentally, means Joanna and the male would be John. At any rate, isn't it strange that members of an immediate family look down on each other? Her other relations back home didn't exactly cherish the idea of her being born at all. Almost sounds like what's going on in America today! She is now an orphan, so to speak. Her husband passed away in 1984 but she is left with two well educated sons both with noted positions in life. She does have a close friend here in Niles, very sisterly, I might add. They communicate with each other on a daily basis. This is what neighbors are for.

She told me when she became a citizen and she gave me the date as February 16,1965. It was absolutely amazing how this woman remembered dates of her life. When she came to America, she said, "I had an excursion ticket." But her return trip was not to be. She came here as a registered nurse, being educated at Ljublanja. After a while, she studied to be a physio-therapist for which she became certified. Believe me, this lady was a worker. She worked as a nurse during the day and at night she would work as an industrial nurse at a factory. Later on when they lived in Niles, she would work in Chicago and come back to Niles on weekends to take care of her family, the house and I suppose the garden. Does anyone wish to volunteer to take up her style of life?

I didn't ask for her age but I do know that she is retired and she's taking summer courses at Brandywine High School. Most of us are looking for summer vacations!

She did give me a geographical location in the town where she was born, namely, Metlika. There was the Kolpa River that ran through the town and this is what divided the Countries of Slovenia and Croatia and this is how I now picture where my parents were born.

She certainly gave me all indications that she loved languages. Ivanka was quite modest when she told me that she speaks Slavonian, Croatian, Italian, Serbian, German, Russian and Polish. Almost sounds like a Litany!

There was a time while living in Niles that she took care of a home for the elderly. Being of foreign extraction, she may not be the most popular person in the neighborhood, but I can tell you this much though, that the friends that she does have are true blue, such as Margaret Albert. I bet this was the first time that she heard the Slavic language!

I could see that she wanted me to sit a while longer as she hurried about the house showing more memories of her life and crying, of course, especially when she talked about not being wanted back home by her family. Margaret saw her crying and I'm sure she heard her cry a thousand times and now it was my turn to see her tears. Don't you wish there was a way to mend broken hearts? For some, hearts are just pumps.

Before I left, she showed me more photos of her prized flower garden and a picture of her tiny outdoor niche bearing a religious figure. She pointed out a painting on the wall of "The Last Supper". There were other paintings, too, that she created but those Twelve Apostles overlooking her dining area were pretty important people in her house. They say that art and music go together so I asked her, "Do you play any instrument?" She answered rather shyly, "I used to play the organ."

I could sense that she knew that I sincerely appreciated anything that had a Slavic taste, namely, books, language, gestures, and things and the last one was a delicacy! For a Croat, it was povatica (apple strudel). What she had taken out of the freezer was a good size serving of a Slovenian dessert and she said, "Here, take." I just had to say, "mnogo hvala." Many thanks.

My memorable visit was complete. I waved and said goodbye in her foreign tongue and I knew that those words brought much joy to this heartsick lady. I knew, too, that by that one painting, that she would never walk alone.

The Hermanns

I must tell you that I have met some very outstanding people in recent times and it was just like finding a cure for a lingering illness. In the course of two years, believe me, I have met some irreplaceable pillars of this city. I can see now that Niles has some of the best citizens in the good ol' U.S. of A. It is so rewarding to walk into a strange house and have your acquaintances, or strangers for that matter, tell you about their life back when they were kids and growing up.

Of course, you know that all this had to start with our immigrants and their offspring such as the one that I am to write about today.

Bob Hermann's parents are immigrants from Hochstberg, Germany. Bob was born in Valls Creek, West Virginia and this is where his father was first employed as a coal miner after he crossed the stormy Atlantic in the early 1900s. Since the parents moved many times, the father, no doubt, must have been a jack of many trades. What is so remarkable about this family is that its lineage can be traced back to the 1600s.

I personally had the opportunity to meet Bob's folks and since I was affiliated with the Niles School System, I had the occasion to meet many of its custodians. I made a special effort to meet Victor Hermann because of his German heritage. You see, back in the late 30s, practically all my professors in high school and Junior college were born and educated in Germany. This is why my visits with this immigrant were that important. There were many things that he told me which also came from the mouths of my educators. The native from Germany had two brothers and a sister that

73

embraced the religious life, one of whom still survives and resides in Sweden. Both of Bob's parents were God-fearing people and the same trait is clearly visible in their offspring.

His spouse, Kay, a member of the Wetmore family, also long known for its Christian bearing, has roots dating back to the early 1800s. She has enjoyed music for many years and I am beginning to wonder if there isn't any inkling of this talent way back and maybe even further than that.

Now, let's delve into the works of this navy man. During my visit, he took me "below deck" and showed me his famous 027 whose railroad yard covers a vast area. This is the second yard that I saw within two weeks. If any of you readers find it difficult to come up with something to do, your best bet is to consult the railroad engineers. The master of 027 really put on a show with his whistle stops, switches, mts., and make-believe people. He told me about his grandson joining him in play, especially when the little one puts on the railroad cap. What camaraderie when the two adults get together and operate each other's set! It's almost like living in the era of the 40s when the Twilight Limited and the Wolverine used to make their excursions from Chicago to Detroit. People tell me that this was indeed the Railroad City of America. Perhaps in the near future I should like to give you a more vivid picture why it was called such a city.

The Hermann family has four daughters and seven grandchildren and I am almost certain that musical shadows will follow these generations.

Many hours of beautiful memories

Gruber's Place

Have you ever walked into a home that was nostalgic? You just have to admit that practically everything you looked at, whether it was resting on a mantel piece or hanging on the wall had a memory of fifty years or more. Of course, an old photo of your parents is priceless and so are the pictures of your children and grandchildren. Looking at such pictures brings me a lot of comfort and pleasure.

Ray Gruber, now a resident of this old railroad town, took great pride in showing me some things that he's been doing since he's been retired. For that matter, even before his last day of work. While he was talking, I was looking. I spotted an old Prince Albert tobacco can and, of course, this brought back memories of my father having such a can and packing his pipe with this choice tobacco. I noticed a small covered wagon with its oxen team all carved by some inmates of Cañon City Prison, Colorado.

Since Ray worked for the Gas Company for many years, he showed me some petrified sand that was found during an excavation just beyond the Niles-Buchanan railroad overpass. These unusual formations were shaped by an underground river.

Do you remember how your parents kept all food stuffs cool? I do know for a fact that these never made their own ice! We had ice men come on certain days to take care of our little problems.

The master of this house evidently knew of someone who took a fancy toward nuts and bolts and built himself an intriguing piece of art. Ray was definitely a do-it-yourselfer. He told me, "I wonder what some people do with themselves once they retire. I hope that they have something to do." I started to twiddle my thumbs when he said that.

This handyman is a native of Cass City, Michigan, a small town located directly east of the dip of the thumb region. His wife, Betty, comes from LaJunta, Colorado, a very famous railroad junction. This is where our young Air Force sergeant met his future spouse. They lived in Colorado for quite some time until they decided to move to Niles. Their two children are currently active in the teaching profession, both of whom still reside in Colorado.

You see, this happy-go-lucky fellow is never bored as he busies himself with a spectacular train lay-out. This is his daily workshop, too. If you ever wish to see a boy in a man, just watch one who owns a train. I tried to remember all the things that I saw within this scale but then I decided to ask you, the reader, what things you have seen on your last train ride. That's what I saw.

As soon as the power was turned on and the switches in order, you'd see the trains going "every which way". It almost made you feel like you wanted to hop on one. Now you know that its conductor was pleased to show me his creation. I wonder how many women out there enjoy this kind of hobby? We do have women engineers on our real trains today so it's very possible that they pilot scale models. It's very possible that our train man started his run because he lived in or around LaJunta, Colorado, handled all sort of trains and where conductors relieved each other on excursion trips. Should you ever visit these beautiful people, don't ever ask the head of the household, "Do you ever get bored now that you're retired?" The people of this city are proud to have them in our midst.

A miniature railroad junction
at Lajunta, Colorado

Andrew Mollison, The Scotsman

Another pillar of our Community is Andrew Mollison. There are indeed many who will vouch that this man has also been a pillar of his Church. We have to travel to the British Isles to locate the birthplace of this tender of legal affairs.

Andy tells me that he was born in Forfar, Scotland some sixty miles north of Edinburgh, the capitol. Knowing that he was a native of the ol' sod, I expected to hear the accent of a Scot, but not so today. This Scotsman knew that I wanted to hear him speak his native tongue and, believe me, I can still hear those R's!

The early Scots of this island were really not involved with the makings of the English language but their cousins from the southern regions were engaged in many skirmishes. England became a melting pot of languages. Dating back to the 5th century there were colonies of Celts, Jutes, Anglo-Saxons, Vikings and Danes that fought for the supremacy of the land, its culture and its language. No doubt these tribes entered this island with their language and left with the influence of other tongues. And so it was with the Roman Missionaries who, came with their Latin influence and in due time, Latin was the language of the Church, Legal matters and of the schools. It wasn't until 1066 that the French became a predominant force in the history of the English language. Prior to that time, the Anglo-Saxons with their crude ways of life were the leaders of the pack. So you see, Mr. Mollison comes to us from a place of much history making.

Andy's father was a machinist by trade at a factory where they produced canvas, linen and jute which eventually was made into bags and then sent throughout the English

Colonies. At this same factory today, carpets are being manufactured. In 1912, his father moved to Glasgow where he worked for Singer Sewing Machine. In 1914, W.W.I broke out and it was at this time that his father worked in the ship building yards in Glasgow. Then came the Great Depression at which time the family moved back to Scotland after the father found employment in the auto industry. After earning enough for a livelihood, the family was once again united at Detroit. This was Andy's first trip to America by ship. He remarked, "That was one trip that I shall never forget. I remember so well going through Ellis Island." In order for them to sail to the New World, there had to be a certain quota of immigrants. From New York, Andy, his mother, and his sister traveled by rail to Detroit to resume their life with Andy's father.

Mr. Mollison worked hard for his education even while attending Southeastern High School in the Motor City. After high school, he attended Detroit Tech where he received his Bachelor of Science in Commerce. While still furthering his education, Andy told me that much of his schooling was in the evening and the day hours were spent in working places such as banks and trust companies. He recalls the days when he walked by the Chrysler Plant which in recent weeks was imploded. This hard working scholar received his law degree at the Detroit College of Law. He was admitted to the Bar in 1940 and just recently received his 50th year membership recognition at the Michigan State Bar Convention.

During my visit with this learned man, I could see a happy person telling all about his life in Scotland and talking about his grandparents and his father's willingness to work. It was very obvious that he, himself, was an ambitious person. His lovely wife, Eve, was not present at our meeting but there was no question that she was a prominent figure in this family circle.

It didn't take long for the head of this household to gather up some information about the family history. "Here, let me show you my grandchildren." he said. You could see that he was abounding in pride. This octogenarian had something to be proud of and besides showing me this pictorial review, he had such high praise for his three sons. One is a lawyer, another an accountant, and the third a journalist in Washington, D.C. I am sure that because of this family's staunch beliefs, the Mollisons have a daughter who is Vicar General of the Sisters of the Congregation of St. Agnes whose Mother House is located at Fond du Lac, Wisconsin.

I was told that a published genealogy of the entire Mollison family is currently being circulated among the clan which includes the sons, daughter, grandchildren and cousins. In this study of family ancestries, so many Americans have lost a desire to inquire about their heritage. Not so with the Mollisons. As Andy was paging through his many memories, he showed me the building where he once practiced much oratory. This was located on Main Street in the Newman Building which is now the Burns and Hadsell Law Office. Since his office was not too distant from his residence, I pictured this young, exuberant lawyer making his daily excursions on foot. No doubt about it, there must be a tug of the heart for this man of much faith as he crosses his path of yesteryear.

Jerry Coughlin

Jerry Coughlin, a resident of our city, remembers something that you and I, in all probability, will never have the occasion to see, namely, the ancient ruins of Rome. As a soldier in World War II in Italy, he also saw the underground cemeteries or tunnels where the early Christians were persecuted and martyred.

This young soldier also saw Mr. Vesuvius whose eruption in 79 A.D. completely buried the city of Pompeii and its surrounding villages. I am sure that all that he had seen he remembered studying back in the Niles High School classroom.

Since Jerry's father was in the Navy, the family had moved several times. They lived in San Diego for a while then decided to move to Niles around 1925. Coming to Niles in a Model T was like blazing a trail. It took them several weeks before they reached this fruit country.

In 1946, he married Betty Cannedy, a native of southern Illinois. The couple was blessed with a son and two daughters. Both their children and grandchildren were raised in staunch religious beliefs.

In the course of our conversation, Jerry told me about the many places of business that once made Niles a very industrial city. A capsule Factory was once in operation at the present site of the playground of the former Westside School. At this plant, margarine was processed. It was the yellow in the capsule that gave the product its final coloration.

He spoke of a place where they made buttons whose material was found on the bottom of the St. Joseph River. It was once called Hose House. Where the Wonderland Store

82

now stands, there used to be a Grey Iron Foundry and at one time, there was a Belt Factory on Wayne and Front Streets.

Jerry had high regard for the late Mr. Skalla for it was he who told Jerry about the many working places in town. It was interesting to learn that there used to be a three-tier bridge south of Fort Street that carried the interurban, a street car and a locomotive. In the course of 70 years, there were three dumping grounds within the city limits. He remembers the ol' Chicago Road when it was mostly gravel and later partially paved to facilitate the horses's climb at Ballard Hill. They say that Island Park was once farmed by a Mr. Weaver. Men used to play Boccie Ball on North Barrett Street. The Italians were good at this game. Jerry was proud to tell me that at one time, he was Dr. Bonine's paperboy, a job he inherited from his predecessor, Paul Weiss. How many of you remember Dr. Yak's Drug Store? It was the building that now staffs the Four Flags Beauty Salon.

I must tell you a few things about Jerry's father. He was a natural at making people laugh and composing music. The grandfather worked as a chef at St. Joseph, Michigan and this is how Jerry's father became a cook at the Four Flags Hotel and also in the Navy.

While being stationed on one of Uncle Sam's submarines in 1916, the older Coughlin nearly lost his life. The sub was in the harbor at New London, Connecticut when it suddenly had taken water and sank, thus entombing 32 young sailors. The ship lay in murky waters for 72 hours before being raised to the surface bringing with it 28 surviving seamen. One of which was Jerry's father. I am sure that during this horrifying ordeal the young sailor thought of all sorts of funny things to say to keep up the morale of his buddies and since he was a music man, this, too, helped to ease the tired minds of the crew.

A destructive and now a peaceful Mt. Vesuvius

Farry's Homestead

Well, here we go again still talking with some beautiful people. You know when you find gold, you keep panning for it. Being with these folks is like listening to a history book. This episode is so real, so human, and this is why I captured it for you.

In the early 1800s, Farry's apple orchard comprised seven acres producing thirty-two varieties of apples. Believe me, this man's "cup runneth over" with stories and I know if we went back, he'd have a few more classics to relate. There came a day when the great-grandfather couldn't get his fire started in the middle of winter so he walked about five miles or so to the old Foster residence to gather up some fire coals. It was a ten mile excursion. Don't you wish that some of these deceased characters would all come to life and replenish the earth with good honest and sound thinking?

A story was told about a relative who owned a good size hog that got into the neighbor's yard. The neighbor thinking that it was a big bear killed it with one shot! Whoever ended up with all that pork, I couldn't say.

Back in '55, the homestead had fifty head of Angus grazing somewhere on the vast acreage. There were three hundred hogs, too, that had to be tended. Besides all the domestic animals, there was the apple orchard that needed care and this is where the Farry children received their primary education. Responsibility and discipline did not come easy. All these cares and concerns paid many dividends, not in monetary value, but in the meaning of a good and sound life.

There was a time when the orchard was taken care of by hired help which was made up of hoboes, Southern whites, the Mexicans, the blacks, the Haitians and Jamaicans. Because of so many cultures, Tom told us that on hot summer nights and early in the fall he would hear them singing their folk songs. "It was like a concert," he added.

There was a school named after this family that took care of eight grades. The building still stands in living memory of educating the Farry clan of four generations. When the school was permanently closed, vandals came in like ruthless scavengers. It became too expensive for repair work and currently stands as "ancient ruins". The school bell, however, now graces the confines of the Farry family. Tom recently celebrated his seventy-eighth birthday, a day on which his son tolled the bell seventy-eight times.

Frances told me about her paternal grandfather's staunch faith. He prayed his rosary daily for countless number of years and after fingering these beads so often, they even showed signs of wear on the side. It could be said that this was an example of a visible living saint.

It happens so often that when you leave your roots, you have a feeling that you'll never see anyone from your old neighborhood, your workplace, your old shopping area, the school you used to attend, the church to which you belonged, just your city. You almost gave up when suddenly this elderly intelligent lady showed up at one of your gatherings. My, my, were you the happy one when she told you that she hailed from Chicago. Not only that, but both of your footsteps were walking the same sidewalks and brushing buildings that you two once did. Frances and Rosemary Flood have cherished each other's friendship since their first meeting.

The sturdy maples and the lofty pines still stand in front of the Ol' Homestead. It seems that after so many years of relaxing, picnicking and visiting under these hardwoods, that these grounds have almost become the hallowed grounds of all the Farrys.

There's a cemetery located in the vicinity that marks the burial place of many descendants of this remarkable family. A 17 ton granite monument gives evidence of a vast lineage.

Tom's dad used to keep his pipe tobacco somewhere off the pantry area. Tom recalls one day when his dad fetched some tobacco, filled his pipe and after a few minutes of delightful smoking, there was a terrific explosion right in front of his face. It was later discovered that while he filled his pipe, he unknowingly put a small .22 caliber shell in the pipe also. Who was blamed for this mishap is still a mystery.

It has happened so many times in this outstanding family, that at any gathering, the grown married children still express their gratitude to their parents for making them what they are. Truly an example of parental and filial love.

Just as we were about to leave, Frances showed us a precious momento that read, "I love you gramma and grampa, I no you love me to." This was a writing that one of the grandchildren had written when he was only six. The grandmother held this treasure closely and said, "I wouldn't give this up for the world."

I have so many beautiful memories of this story that I best tell you before "all the bridges are down", as there is no turning back. This was an experience that my wife and I will cherish for the remainder of our lives.

Do you remember the story that I told you about the Eau Claire bandits that were in cahoots with the law? Well, a few miles east of a tamarack swamp, the place where they nailed the cops, stands a mammoth maple tree. This is the setting for today's narrative.

I would like to have you meet some good old fashioned people who are the owners of this remarkable landmark. May I introduce you to Tom and Frances Farry.

Since Tom is a native of this little town, he'll tell us more about this crooked and doctored up maple. He was pretty proud to tell me that this once sturdy hunk of wood is about 125 years old. Surrounding this oldie, there are other oldies such as other lofty maples and towering whispering pines. I can tell you this much, that if their Maker designed them to speak, what stories they could tell!

By the way, Tom does recall the excitement at the Eau Claire Bank when the good guys were shootin' it out with the bad guys. Tom was only nine then and he's still living in the same old house where he was born which is 150 years old. A few alterations and additions still make this place a beautiful warm home. The original Farry Homestead, the one with the great-grandparents is still weathering the many storms dating back to 1835. Isn't it absolutely striking that one's brain, an intricate piece of creation, is able to relate to us something that happened many, many years ago?

The lineage of this hardworking family goes back to around 1835, perhaps even further, if it were not for the carelessness of discarding the Holy Bible which in so many families carries it weight in gold. Like many families, years of precious ancestry had been recorded only to have it destroyed after some senseless argument. In spite of all that took place, the present family possesses an enviable culture.

My wife and I visited these warm people on Wednesday, December 18, 1991 and what a gorgeous setting for a Christmas card - it snowed heavily and the entire landscape was covered by a new blanket of snow. A country lunch was prepared for us and this is where my story began. We sat, talked and laughed for four hours. So all the thoughts I give to you this day were all given to me by Tom and Frances Farry.

The Farrys were married in Chicago in '49, at the home of the bride. This notable courtship began during Tom's confinement in an Army General Hospital where Frances was employed. You see, Tom was wounded in England during W.W.II. and returned to the United States for recovery. The couple was blessed with five children; one daughter and four sons all of whom live "within reach". The home today is like Grand Central Station with all the grandchildren. There have been times when the house would be occupied overnight by 40 family members.

When we first walked into the living room, I noticed five Christmas stockings lined up along the staircase which gave evidence that five siblings were raised in this family circle. I was told later that Frances' aunt made these memorable decorations back in 1950.

Back at the lunch table, Tom was telling us that in 1835 an acre of land was purchased for 25¢. Tom's great-grandfather came to America from Ireland when he was 32 years old with 25¢ in his pocket. Tom asked me, "Would you like to see his baggage?" I knew it was going to be something old looking but I didn't realize that it would be that small. Here are its dimensions: 14 inches long, 8 inches wide and 8 inches deep. It was a miniature trunk in which he carried all his belongings! From what I gathered, it was close to 200 years old and surely showing signs of deterioration and an excellent hideout for the rodent family. The interior of this antique was lined with old newspapers and Tom's only regret is that he should have been aware of this years ago. The mice had other ideas!

When the 32 year old came to this country, he wore out a lot of shoe leather looking for work. He did stop at a farmer's house and the farmer put him to work pronto. He took him to the field and said to the new recruit, "See that rock pile over there? Throw all the rocks over the fence and when you're finished with that, throw them back." The young man did exactly what he was told and because there was no quarrel, the farmer gave him a permanent job.

Story has it that when Tom's great-grandmother lived near the present sight, she noticed an Indian approaching the house one day motioning that he was hungry. It was just a matter of minutes when she handed him a loaf of bread that

89

was cut lengthwise and smothered in butter. The most inspiring aspect about this meeting is that the Indian returned a few weeks later carrying a hind quarter of venison for her.

At one time, the great grandfather owned 1250 acres which he eventually gave to his kin. Some prospered by it and others squandered their holdings.

The Island of Malta

Some time ago I told you that we would be meeting a little lady from the tiny island of Malta. Just last week I informed you that we'd be traveling there, so pack your bags and let's go. Our imaginary trip to this piece of land in the Mediterranean Sea would take about 8 hours from Chicago to Rome and then an additional 1½ hours to our final destination, Malta.

Before we meet this lady, let me first tell you a little about this island. It is indeed a small stretch of land about 60 miles south of Sicily and south of Italy. It is ancient, historic, picturesque, environmentally warm throughout the year, and very strategic. I will tell you more in a moment but now let's meet this person with a thousand remarkable memories.

Her name is Olga Maria Domenica Fiorini. Before you read on, you must go back over those names again and be sure that you roll your r's as this is what makes the pronunciation more romantic. She was born in Valetta, the capital of Malta. This seaport was named after Jean Parisot de La Valetta, Grand Master of the Knights of Malta in 1580. Her roots were aristocratic. Her mother was the granddaughter of a baroness. Both her parents were of Italian descent. Her father came from Florence, Italy and her mother was a Maltese. Being that they were among the elite, they had three servants whose names were Romio and two sisters, Katherine and Anna. Her father would often say, "You know that Romio is so ugly, but I love him so." I wish that you, the reader, would have been present to see her give this presentation. This is precisely why I have undertaken this writing bit, as people, at least the ones I have spoken to, are beautiful human beings and today's books do not especially elaborate about.

I truly wish that I could display her foreign artistic script. Personally, it thrills me. Malta, she says, is independent now and an opera-loving country. Its people love music and the opera and, of course, the island is steeped in Renaissance. The sport fans, as you might have guessed, are passionately interested in soccer. Her father was a prominent importer, as most of the island's commodities were imported. Her mother's aunt, Contessa Falirmo Navarra (go back and roll the r's) became Countess by inheritance. Believe it or not, during this time, too, she was flashing photos of her kin handling them like a deck of cards. The people on the island that compromised the population were from Italy, France, Germany and Poland and after so many centuries, they all became Maltese. Olga attended a Catholic school called Marghirita Di Savoia. All her religious doctrine was taught by nuns. Roman Catholicism is the state religion of Malta.

Olga Maria Domencia tells about two earthquakes that hit the island. The first struck in 1919 while she and her sister were practicing piano with their maestro. It was at this time that all the walls came tumbling down upon them. The second disaster came in 1925 and this is when their father said, "Come now, it's time to move." So the family left for Tunis in North Africa where her father continued with his import business which was quite lucrative, I might add.

As she described her residence, she gestured, "We could see a castle very clearly from the third story of our terrace." She very legibly and artistically gave me the names of her immediate family both living and deceased. She may have hesitated a bit as to all their ages but here they are nevertheless: Joseph Gregory, the father; Maria Stella Marino Gioria, the mother (now both deceased); Michael, 85 and still alive; and Mario, 58 who currently resides in Florida. These are all brothers. The sisters are Matilda, now deceased;

Beatrice, 83; and our Olga, now 82. All the living, with the exception of Michael, reside on the island. Those deceased are all buried in Malta.

Olga's brother, Gregory, a Franciscan priest, is retired and is now living in Malta. Father Bonaventura, as he is now called because of his religious order, was a writer for 53 years at the Vatican. He wrote for the L'Osservatorio Romano, a Vatican newspaper which told the world what was going on at the Vatican. He once had the occasion to brush shoulders with our present spiritual leader, Pope John Paul II. The priest spoke in Latin, English, Italian, French and Maltese. His sister tells us that he was a happy-go-lucky man yet serious and he loved to eat! While his parents still lived in Tunis, he called them back to live again on the island. After their deaths, he arranged that they be buried in the plot that he had reserved for them and this is where he also wishes to be buried.

I learned that everybody in Malta loves music and singing. It seems that everyone who has a good voice sings and this was without much training. They were naturals. When Olga came to America, she sang at concerts at New York City. She distinctly remembers singing at a National Jamboree in Washington, D.C. in 1936. In the group were Americans and Polish troops. It was around this time that she married a German diplomat. When he returned to his native country, he never returned. Olga is almost convinced that the War was responsible for his failure to return. She did give birth to a daughter, Maria, who also lives in the vicinity.

She also spoke of a brother and a group of university students who came to America in 1925 and later became the editor of an Italian newspaper in New York City. Olga became a citizen in 1945. The University of Malta became the home of many worldwide generals, for this is where most of them were educated. She took much pride in telling me this. Besides her love for music, languages were her second love.

These are English, Italian, French and Maltese. While living on the island, she recalls studying music and languages. On Saturday afternoons, her mother would take her to the opera when she was only 10. Every evening, her family would all come together to recite the Rosary. This was a must.

There is so much history connected with Maltese people. For those of you who are not familiar with catacombs, they are underground tunnels and hiding places for the early Christians, prisoners and generals. Malta still has them. The island is considered an exceptionally strategic point on the European Continent.

Olga goes on to say that her mother was a very charitable person. She always helped the British troops, especially those who were wounded. She specialized in making raisin cake and this is what she fed them and the prisoners.

From our study of European history, all of us know that Napoleon Bonaparte was hungry for land as were so many other past leaders. On his list, was also the beautiful island of Malta. He did land there in the early 1800s but with the help of the British, the Maltese put an end to that siege. Even as far back as 1565, the scrappy sword-wielding Knights of Malta freed the island from the ever ravaging Turks. Somewhere in the annals of the Maltese history, it is said that in 60 A.D., St. Paul the Apostle was shipwrecked near the island. Evidently, he was on his way there to Christianize the inhabitants.

Poland

Today I had the pleasure of talking to Dor Rodolak, a native of Lodz, Poland. She came from a family of eight children; three sisters and five brothers. Her father had a big farm with many horses, cows, sheep, turkeys, chickens and geese. They lived about five miles from the city. Besides having all this livestock, her father operated a flour mill.

The city of Lodz was a great manufacturing place. More so than Gdansk, which was an outstanding seaport. Being that her birthplace was located in the middle of Poland, other large cities were almost equidistant from her town.

Dora told me that school and education were very important. They had classes six days a week and she especially remembers when the teachers would unload hours of homework for the weekend.

"Our family was always healthy and we never went to see a doctor as long as I can remember. I often pictured my father working on the farm with his horses and plow. So many of the people there were hard-working. Things were quite primitive for a long time and then as time went on, you could see that things were improving a little. We often prayed together. There was no question that our Catholic faith was very strong and I am proud to say that it still is in Poland. Shortly after I was married, my husband became a teacher and it was his duty to teach all subjects."

"As I sit here and tell you about myself, my father, my friends and my church," Dora exclaims, "I wish I could tell you everything but I am so heart sick about so many things."

"But I will tell you something," she says with her Polish accent, "The thing we had to do was to get out of our big farm house. The only thing we could take with us is that which we could carry on our backs. All the farm animals had to stay on the premises. Now where to go? It seems like it was everybody for himself. We had to find some shelter. After a while, one was here, the other was here, some were there and so on. All our dreams of continuing a happy life were indeed shattered. It was almost a nightmare that we had to move. The SS Troops took over the whole city and now we had to live under constant fear. I learned later that one of my brothers was killed by them and so was my husband after hiding in many, many places.

"When the troops arrived, their main objective was to capture and seize the rich, their jewelry, their money, their land and whatever they had of value. We learned, too, that all our records of baptism, marriages and deaths were all destroyed giving some evidence of the beginnings of a superior race. Our faith and our church was now being tested. At this moment, I am certainly not proud to tell you that I didn't see the inside of a church for five years for this is how long they kept me away. I felt that we were constantly being chased like rabbits. We would continue somehow to keep up our religious gathering underground. The church we once attended and all the other churches were now being used as warehouses for the Army's ammunitions dump. They used to store hay in there also. All places of worship were now desecrated.

"There was countless numbers in this city of wealth who fell prey to the looters. It was just a matter of time that thousands of people were being transported to a concentration camp at Ravensbrik, Germany. It was estimated that 40,000 women were hauled into this camp which was comprised of varied nationalities. It was a happy moment in some sort of way that when the Russians came, we were shattered. As I told you earlier in my story, I wish I could tell you more in detail, but then I would more or less begin to relive a horror story. After the freedom, I moved to Sweden. Being with so many different peoples, I learned many languages such as Russian, Polish (of course), German, Slovak, Swedish, and English. In telling you my account, I do know for certain that when the troops took me, they gave me a mark that will be on my person all my life."

"I was fortunate to be able to move to the United States in 1958. It wasn't too long after that, that I was hired by the French Paper Company, here in Niles where I worked for 28 years. I am now retired and ever so grateful for all the blessings I received.

"Just recently, I visited a Catholic school in Lapeer, Michigan where my daughter is a piano teacher. I talked to several eighth graders about my life in Poland and they left me with some beautiful momentos, one of which I wish to share with you. It reads like this, "Thank you for telling us about your life. It was wonderful to know that you never stopped believing in God. I really admire your faith in God. Thank you again. Love, Alice L.

"Since I came to America, I have had a fruitful life. I have had many nice friends, cared for my big beautiful garden and gone to church often. Since my brother's children and my friends still live in Poland, I often send them many gifts and much clothing. I feel this is the least that I can do for those whose blood is identical to mine and for those who have wished me well and have prayed for me for so many years. To the reader, thank you for listening to me."

Quest for Freedom

My spouse, who is also of Polish extraction, often speaks of her father, John Miswick (anglicized from the original Misiewicz). He was born in Kielce, Poland on May 8, 1887. He came from a large family and at an early age, he became a tool and die maker which later brought him much success in America. His children have stated that he also was a talented pianist. Because of this artistic trait, they, too, plus his grandchildren, and great grandson, either by piano, voice or just a keen musical perception, have inherited this special natural ability.

Back in Poland, when John was a young man, the Russians and Germans were on the prowl again and this young Pole was a draft potential. For this reason, he fled the confines of his hometown. After fleeing and hiding for two or three years, he finally made his way to the seaport at Bremen, Germany. This was in October, 1907. It was there that he embarked on the ship S.S. Cassel and sailed for New York. They say that he often spoke of his voyage being very frightening because of the heavy seas.

When he settled here in America, he married Helen Botwinski at Knowlton, Wisconsin on September 5,1911. They made their home in Niles shortly after their marriage and it was at National Standard that he continued his trade as machinist.

During his early life in Niles, his mother corresponded with his wife for a few years informing him and his family how things were back in Poland.

His quest for freedom became ultimate when he took the Oath of Allegiance on November 27, 1942.

War Clouds Over Croatia

Back in the late 1800s, steamers were carrying European immigrants over the stormy Atlantic. Every ocean liner just before its docking at New York Harbor, had to stop at Ellis Island where its passengers were to be inspected by customs officials. These weary travelers came from Finland, Sweden, Denmark, Italy, Germany, France, the Slavs from Poland and Yugoslavia, and the English from Cornwall, England. Most of the immigrants had passports stamped for the Upper Peninsula of Michigan, more precisely, the Copper Country. This was Boom Town, U.S.A. This was the land of rich copper finds.

In that bunch of trail blazers was my father, a young and newly married man. His wife, who in time became my mother, followed some months later. It was during this interval that my father found employment and a home for his family.

Both of my parents were born in the village of Lokve which, over the years, was known to be Gorski Kotar. They were Croats from Croatia and they spoke the Croatian language which is the tongue that I first learned and since then have retained.

In their birthplace, they worked, played and prayed. The country's terrain was hilly and mountainous. There were many tiny communities that outlined the valleys such as the ones we see pictured on our television screens. Each family then had a few domestic animals and a garden.

In recent times, I have been moved by all the transactions that have taken place in the Slavic regions as I vividly recollect my parents telling me their home, their land

and their place of worship. I can still remember my father talking about different localities which our news announcers daily disclose.

The Civil War, which has besieged the countries of Croatia, Bosnia Hercegovina and Serbia, has brought much grief and consternation to millions of people. Some form of hatred and ill will has prevailed in this nation for hundreds of years and it is only in the recent past that the United Nations' troops have revealed to the rest of the world about the mass killings, the rapes, the slaughtering and butchering of mankind. It was Slav against Slav and brother against brother. Perhaps before the end of the this so-called ethnic cleansing, more villages, towns, communities and cities will be completely annihilated. We may yet see not the truckloads of the living, but the remains of the dead.

Thirty years have passed since the death of my parents and had they been living to read, see and listen to what is taking place in, near and around their homeland, I wonder whether they would have been able to withstand the shocking sights of war. There was a time when I corresponded with my cousins but for some unknown reason, this writing ceased to be. At present, I often ponder about their fate and even think that in their situation, they may be mortal enemies. For a while, different religious and beliefs fought hand in hand and now it is to each his own. My only regret at the moment is that I never curiously inquired about my brother's visit to that little town of our parents' birth. But I can easily envision his visits with relatives whom he has never seen. He undoubtedly walked the roads and paths that were once used by our parents. I am sure that he cherished the memory of being with his fellow-Croats.

It is rather ironic that in recent years, thousands of pilgrims visit the site where the Mother of our Lord appears frequently to some very special and privileged people. It is on the rocky hillside at Medjugorje that visitors from all parts of the world come to pray for health, happiness and especially for peace while on the other side of this mountain range, there is much bloodshed.

Since the fighting has been escalated, I seem to be confused about the actions of the various ethnic groups. With the fall of Communism, there came a very noticeable change and it was obvious that one of the Yugoslav provinces sought to be in sole command.

In the beginning of this armed strife, we saw the Dalmation Coast being battered and shelled mercilessly, destroying ancient structures that held invaluable historical facts dating back to 200 B.C. I certainly recall my father describing the beauty of this Adriatic Coastline.

At this point, I wish to bring to mind the life of a renowned historian, Fr. Victor Rogulj. He was a native of Dalmatia, born in 1897. His classical studies took place in Ljubljana, the capital of Slovenia. He studied his philosophy on the island of Cres, located in the northern Adriatic. He completed his theological studies at the University of Innsbruk in Austria and eventually was ordained a priest in 1921. While a student at the University, he became well versed in languages. Besides his Croatian language, he spoke German and Latin fluently. In 1939, he became pastor of our Croatian parish in Calumet, Michigan and it was here that I, too, developed a love for languages. Since the mother tongue of my parents was a dialect, it was our pastor that taught me the correct usage. During my visits with him, he often spoke Latin. Incidentally, he spoke the English language flawlessly though with a pronounced foreign accent. I am ever so grateful to this scholar for giving me a deeper insight into the history of his land which, at the moment, is being torn apart by Moslems, Croats, Bosnians and Serbs.

I was saddened by the death of this learned and saintly man. He was laid to rest in a country that he loved so well. Those that knew him and touched him were blessed a hundred-fold. I am certain that had he lived to hear and see what was done to the ancient grounds at Dalmatia, the human frailty of man would have been easily displayed. I couldn't say how much he would have endured watching busloads of refugees fleeing from the enemy, watching relatives exchanging notes and hugs, listening to long-lost brothers, watching mothers meeting up with their children. Every scene is a story in itself.

Television is giving us a daily picture of scared people scurrying from one street corner to another, of people carrying knapsacks, perhaps their life's belongings, of all kinds of life riding in and on rigs, packed like sardines. Just running away from the snow, the cold, the freezing temperatures and from their fellow man, their enemy. One could see a few tears of joy but most were tears of sorrow. Television also showed us desperate ham radio operators trying to answer the pleas in the next valley, in their Slavic tongue, "Will someone please do something, will someone please help us."

Where once the Winter Olympics were held in Sarajevo, now people run in fear. Where men were once seen sipping their Turkish coffee, and enjoying a sip of Slivovica. Now that they are being pounded by artillery shells, they huddle in their basements still puffing at their cigarettes and having their afternoon coffee or better still a drink of homemade brew and ever mindful of the enemy that lurks in the streets above. And if I were there, I would come back and tell you exactly what was said. Surely, it wouldn't be pleasant.

Paul Harvey, one of America's noted radio news commentators, recently remarked that at present, there are 73 places in the world steeped in some kind of trouble, some nations at war, some in tension and some in want. There are so many places in Yugoslavia that are showing the scars of war, and there are places that are no more. All along the valleys, you will see the names of Vitez, Tuzla, Bosnia

Hercegovina, Croatia, Zuti, Sarajevo and Srebrenica. I am forever hoping and praying that my kinfolk and the people living in and around those tiny villages will someday soon be given the sign of peace.

Christmas In Europe

For the next four weeks or so, I would like to share with you some Christmas traditions from foreign lands. In so doing, I hope that it will make your Holiday season a bit more meaningful and joyful. At the end of each segment, they will wish you Christmas and New Years Greeting and Felicitations in their foreign tongue.

Today, may I introduce the peoples of Finland and Slovenia:

Christmas In Europe

Some months ago, Ivanka Ritter told us about the time she helped her father cook for 30 workers in his vineyard. She was only ten years old then. This same little girl wishes to tell our readers what Christmas was like back in Metlika, a small town in Slovenia, one of the Republics of Yugoslavia. Most Europeans are blessed to have a day like St. Nicholas Day on December 6. This saint was their Santa Claus.

On this special day of the year, St. Nicholas, with two of his helpers, would go about the villages and reward all the good children. There would always be someone who would dress up as a bishop, representing the saint, and one of his helpers was disguised as a devil, who took care of those that were bad. The bishop would ask the children if they were bad. He would also ask the children if they knew their prayers, and those that did, were given candy and other goodies and the less fortunate were given pieces of coal. It so happened on this day that Ivanka became ill, perhaps being afraid of the visiting cleric. Her father comforted her, though, and she did become frightened when they heard that he was in town, as they knew that he would ask them questions.

Shortly after this celebration, Ivanka's mother began her Christmas baking. Much of what she made were cookies and walnut cake which was given to their many friends in the community. Since money was so scarce, this took the place of material things. She remembers the days when they would chop down the Christmas tree. When the snow was deep, her father would hitch up the team of horses to a sleigh and get the tree. When there wasn't any snow, they all walked to the woods. Ivanka remarked that this was the time of the year when many poor people respected each other and possessed all the riches in the world!

Her family started decorating the tree around December 20. Their people followed a custom called Badnik which meant that all adults of a certain age would uphold the laws of Fast and Abstinence. They all attended Midnight Mass at the parish church and when they returned, they all sipped at some hot wine and ate povatica which resembled a strudel. Another custom among the Slavic people was that they made many sweet breads. On one of which were placed little animals made out of dough. After the bread was baked, her father would cut a few slices and give it to his farm animals. He would return from church with a container full of holy water then take a goose feather, dip it in the blessed water and bless his livestock. Whether this custom still persists, I do not know.

For the big Christmas Day celebration, Ivanka's parents and their guests would have a roasted piglet that was made at an outdoor rotisserie. In the animal's cavity, you would find green onions, potatoes, parsley, apples, and bits of bacon. Being that her father was the master winemaker, there was much cheer with his home-made vintage. Since there were many poor people living in that vicinity, Ivanka's family often made dinners for those who were in need. This lady of much concern wishes all of you to have Vesele Bozicne Praznike!

Christmas in Finland

It is the most important festival of the year. I know this to be a fact as I personally have lived with many Finnish immigrants in the Upper Peninsula. Santa Claus doesn't live too far from Finland and that's because Lapland is Santa's home.

Ed and Marie Kangas from Buchanan sent me some literature about Christmas in Finland for which I am ever so grateful. Ed's roots are in Negaunee where his parents made their home after coming from Finland. The high point of a Finnish Christmas is the singing of songs in Finnish on Christmas Eve. As a rule, there is always a white Christmas in Finland. The smell of the tree and the glow of candles, the presents and food are also a big part of this season.

On December 13, the Swedish speaking Finns celebrate the Feast of St. Lucia. She was a Sicilian saint who suffered martyrdom and on this date, the Finnish people celebrate it with great dignity. Another tradition that these Europeans have is the "Tierna boys" who, according to custom, go from house to house sort of begging for money to help with their college tuition.

One of the Yuletide dishes that they are noted for is the gingerbread and also "pulla" which is a pastry consumed during coffee time. Speaking of coffee time, the Finns consume the most coffee in the world. Besides their everyday coffee, special "coffee" occasions include birthday coffee, name day coffee, engagement coffee, wedding coffee, funeral coffee, baptism coffee and graduation coffee. These are all served with biscuits, buns and cakes.

The main dish with these northern people is the Christmas ham. The eating of ham is the last surviving relic of the ancient Scandinavian sacrificial rite. This coincides with the sacrifice of a pig to Frejia, the goddess of love and fertility. The Christmas season ends on January 6, the day of Epiphany, the Feast of the Three Kings or the Wisemen or the Magi.

Together, with my many Finnish friends, may we wish all of you A Iloista Joulua.

Christmas in Slovakia

I was so pleased to receive a letter from Pittsburgh, Pennsylvania, the home of Mrs. Mary Zatko and her daughter, Mrs. Millie Young the former of which once lived in Niles together with her son, the late Fr. James Zatko. Mary Zatko is an immigrant from Slovakia and it was her daughter that gave me some beautiful thoughts about Christmas in this European country. I am sure that there are many people in our community who knew this family to be great historians. It was their son, Fr. James, who was a professor of History at St. Mary's College in Notre Dame, Indiana.

The customs that these Slavic people possess really express the joy and hope that they feel at the birth of Jesus Christ. Christmas, as they put it, meant a bountiful evening. It was the most custom-filled day of the Christmas season. They have many special foods and activities at the evening meal. The mother or father would make a small sign of the cross on the foreheads of everyone present. This gesture reminds all Christians to have Christ in their thoughts at all times and to live and work in such harmony and pleasant fellowship that will sweeten all their lives. It also may have symbolized that the love between husband and wife stay as sweet as honey, likewise the love of a child toward its parents and to be loved by others accordingly. The main meal would begin with Oplatky, an unleavened wafer which has nativity scenes imprinted on it. The father serves this with honey to everyone present.

One great custom among the European Slovaks was that carolers went about singing in the neighborhood and while doing so, they would be called into the homes where they would be given all sorts of pastries and delicacies prepared for this season.

Another custom practiced was the Bethlehem Strollers who went about visiting homes displaying a miniature Bethlehem scene. As this was done, there was much seasonal song and dance.

Of course, Christmas for children began on December 6, The Feast of St. Nicholas. Children would leave their shoes on door sills to have St. Nick fill them with candy, toys, fruits and books. They, too, would partake of the unleavened Oplatky asking Our Lord to be with them throughout life's journey.

The nice people from Pittsburgh and the many Slovaks from Niles wish everyone Vesele Vianaci.

Christmas in Poland

I wanted to learn what Christmas was like in Poland. Some months ago, Dora Podolak, an immigrant from that very God-fearing country gave me her harrowing experiences as a young girl. Today, with the help of her niece, who recently arrived from Poland, she told me about Christmas back home.

From our TV viewing, we are certainly convinced that Poland is predominantly Catholic and its people have practiced their faith to the letter. The first thing she told me about this season was, "There is very much praying." Many people made their own ornaments as they were very imaginative and creative. She informed me that parents didn't want their children to play too much but instead wanted them to read and learn music. Little wonder then that this country produced many clerics, musicians and learned men and women.

One custom that just about every Pole practiced, was that each home displayed a bale of hay underneath the dining room table with an immaculate tablecloth. This symbolized the birth of the Infant Jesus in Bethlehem.

She told me that on Christmas Eve, no one was to eat supper until the first star appeared in the heavens. In preparing the food this day, no grease was to be used, as here, too, the law of Fast and Abstinence was observed.

Christmas in Croatia

Since I am an offspring of immigrant parents from Croatia, Yugoslavia, I will try to share with you all the thoughts we had at Christmas in our household.

To begin with, Christmas was indeed a very holy time of the year. We talked about it for four weeks as this was Advent Season. I do not recall our Christmas being material. Since money was so scarce, many things were made.

A balsam or spruce tree would always be the proverbial Christmas tree. It would be chopped a day or so before the Eve. When I became of age, this was my chore and I enjoyed it to the fullest and this is what I still miss during the month of December.

Our tree back home was always decorated promptly at 6 p.m. December 24. This was my mother's custom and her wish. We had an old pendulum clock and when the chimes sounded 6, it was time to "clear the deck". My mother would be at the controls and everything that she put on that tree was placed expertly and meticulously.

There is no question that it was truly a sublime moment. Having lighted candles on the tree was a custom back then, but a dangerous one. Gifts were few and those that were visible were homemade, such as mittens, wool socks, scarves and caps. Going to church at midnight was really the climax to our Christmas.

Since all the Slavs in our little colony had small farms, our Christmas meals consisted of pork, beef and chicken. For dessert, we had our famous kolac and povatica. There were other many sweet breads that enhanced our feast.

Being of European descent, these people also followed the great custom of having St. Nicholas visit all the homes. I do remember so distinctly when I, too, put my shoe on the window sill to have St. Nick fill it with candies. There were times that my shoe did have rocks and bit of coal!

Another custom that I recall was visiting the neighborhood and having the people place coins in the meat of the apple then go home and count your reward.

On New Year's Day, the main meal was headcheese which was made from the feet of the pig. Our Christmas season came to an end on January 6 which was the Feast of the Three Kings. This is when our tree was taken down. It was a time when we were so grateful for the little things that we received. From our household to yours, Sretan Bozic!

Christmas In Hungary

I had the pleasure of listening to Mr. and Mrs. Laszlo Vesei, Hungarian immigrants to this country in 1943. According to the head of this household, there were many customs in this country. The most interesting of which were the travels of St. Nicholas. He was the patron saint of sailors, travelers, bakers, merchants, and especially children. He lived in the 300s.

They say that on the Eve of St. Nicholas, many young adults dressed up as bishops and those that accompanied him were the devils called Krampus. The children were often asked how well they knew their prayers and, of course, many were fearful of what would happen if they did not know some answers. Those that did not fare well, were not given anything edible but were given pieces of coal by the two "devils".

110

Mr. Vesei followed this same custom with his children when they were younger. Usually, here in America, the children would put some form of footwear on the window sills or at some other designated area.

Still another custom that began on December 13 is St. Lucy's Day. On this day, boys would start building a stool until it was completed on December 24 when they took it church on Christmas Eve.

During the elevation of the host, they would stand on this stool and look about to see if they could capture the eyes of some girl which was the sign of marriage in the future. The girls would also try it with the boys. Even the thought of death was exercised. During this "holy" season, the boys would dress up as shepherds carrying a little church which they built and in it were the Infant Jesus and the Mother Mary.

With this assembly, they would visit the neighborhood and receive monies.

The children were not permitted to see the tree until Christmas Eve when it was completely decorated. On this day, the meal was meager because their people followed the strict rules of Fast and Abstinence. Their meal consisted of sauerkraut soup with mushrooms, sliced hard boiled eggs and finally fried fish. The meal ended by everyone eating some kolac. Of course, attending Mass on the Eve or Christmas Day was in order. The meal on Christmas was a scrumptious pork roast with all the trimmings.

On New Year's Eve, an occasion for much drinking, someone would bring along a live piglet and if the animal squealed after you pinched it, that was a sign of good luck. The next day, that same piglet was roasted with an apple in its mouth.

Like so many other Christian European countries, Christmas came to an end on January 6 at the Feast of the Three Wisemen.

These nice people from Hungary wish all of you Kellemes Karacsonyt!

B.U.E.K. Boldog Ujevet Kivanou.

Pearl Harbor

About 46 ships of the Pacific Fleet dropped anchor in Pearl Harbor during the month of December. This was their resting place so to speak. On December 7, 1941, at 7:55 a.m., they were like sitting ducks in a pond ready to be "picked off" by the hunters.

This naval base, "the pond", I am sure, had been under surveillance for days, for weeks, for months and, perhaps, even for years. By 10 a.m. or so, this harbor was almost erased from the Hawaiian Islands. Here are some stories as told to me by some of our local survivors. One of the accounts was given to me by my nephew from Milwaukee, Wisconsin, hence the chief reason for my writing about this holocaust.

Wilfred Bozick, my nephew, was 20 years old when Uncle Sam grabbed him and put him on the Battleship Nevada. He tells me that he was getting ready to clean up and change into his dress whites. Standing guard at the raising of the colors was his buddy, Zakrewski from Greendale, Wisconsin. This is when all hell broke loose. What could a few armed men with rifles do against waves of machine gunning Zeroes?

Black smoke was beginning to billow from the ships and some thought they were mistakenly hit by their own planes. Not so, this was real enemy bombardment. The call to battle stations sent young, frightened Bozick to his post high in the forward mast of the Nevada. As he climbed to his station, he saw many planes flying right over his head.

He remembers saying, "I think I climbed four rings at a time instead of two. Some planes came in smokestack level." They all knew it was the Japanese as they could easily see the "red ball" on the wings. Now that he reached the top, the young navyman had an excellent view of the Harbor. The USS Nevada was the only ship that could get out of there for a while. But before the Japanese nailed her with three torpedoes and several bombs, her skipper beached her near the entrance to the Harbor.

"The Arizona just blew up," he said. "I could see men jumping off the masts. Some hit the deck and others jumped into the fiery waters. A thousand men died instantly. I tried to hide like a hunted rabbit."

Franky Frucci, a lifelong resident of Niles, and once mayor of this Four Flags city was stationed at Hickman Field when the Zeroes hit. "We could almost touch them, that's how close they were." According to Airman Frucci, all the planes on the Field were either destroyed or crippled and were useless for retaliation. His buddy from Kalamazoo, Bernie, yelled out, "Let's go to church." Most of the airmen were just getting out of bed when the enemy hit. The planes made several passes at the Field, strafing everything and everyone in sight. He remembers welders using torches trying to get at some of the men trapped in ships, but this particular process stole the oxygen, thus suffocating them.

Another serviceman from Niles was John P. Orias, who was at the submarine base when all this took place. John has since passed away, but his sister told me that he was on a ladder doing some repair work when bullets started flying. Somehow by good fortune, his brother Joseph stationed on the USS Concord had been anchored at Pearl Harbor a day or so before the attack, but his ship was ordered for open waters and thus avoiding the inferno.

The first Niles casualty of WWII was Fred Amon, who was on the ill-fated Arizona. The Amon family suffered another loss, as a brother, Cleland, of the Air Force was shot down by the Germans on a mission over the oil fields of Ploesti, Romania.

According to a statement issued by Cletus Schuh, his brother, Walter, now deceased, was also at Pearl Harbor on the USS Monterey which was tied next to the Arizona when he saw it completely destroyed by a volley of bombs, torpedoes and strafing.

Young Bill Wenger, Chief Radioman on the battleship USS Hull explained to me his ordeal on the December morning. Like most men on a ship that was anchored or being pounded, it was absolute chaos. He traded work detail that day and while having breakfast and getting ready for church services, this day of many deaths and much suffering took place. Only those that were there can best describe what took place. "There was much shooting, many dying, many wounded and many dead." "I was scared stiff and this is the day I grew up very quickly," Bill remarked. He also continued, "It was our training and discipline that really helped us to realize the pain of mind and body." I could tell by listening to him that he was indeed proud to salute Old Glory.

Jack Stanner, the Marine Bulger, was getting reedy to go on watch at Ewa, a Marine air base. "The sight was absolutely sickening," Jack said. He remembers these new F4F fighters which the Air Force received were all lined up, burnt hulks.

"First night after the attack," Jack states, "was really spooky and rumors flying so fast and thick that you could walk on them. I can still see the smoldering wreckage."

There was a man from the US Infantry 27th Division from Niles who tells us about that Day of Infamy. John Demos says, "It is still so vivid, very true never to be forgotten and still like yesterday." He tells us that he was in bed sleeping and his "Kopkick" came in and yelled, "Come on you Budda Heads, this is the real McCoy." John said, "We had to kick in the Arsenal door to get at the ammo. I remember picking up machine guns from my fallen comrades. Sometimes it was hard to see the Japanese bombers as the sun was in our eyes. Ammunition was so scarce that at one time, we were throwing potatoes at low flying planes." This was sheer desperation.

He told me he can't forget the moment when he tried to save a little girl who had just been strafed. He, too, was wounded in this attempt and after being "patched up", his bunch was ready for a complete invasion by the Japanese which never came. "Had this been the case," John said, "The Japanese flag would be flying today on the Hawaiian Islands."

Alex Evanovich, a Navy fireman on the Destroyer, USS Worden, talked to me at length about the happenings at Pearl Harbor. He remembers too well about that catastrophe. For a moment, I thought I noticed his eyes becoming a bit watery, as if he was about to shed a tear. Had he done this, it would have been very natural as he was talking about war and death. What he said and how he said it could have baffled many journalists.

We exchanged a few personal thoughts as his father, a native of Serbia, spoke practically the same Slavic tongue as my father. We even talked in Serbian and Croatian. After we spoke about our ancestral countries, he opened up about the savagery of war. He remembers being in the fireroom when the bombing began and he was up and down those stairs like a mad man. Alex told me what the Japanese used to torpedo bombers, dive bombers and high altitude bombers. He recalls the tender ship, USS Bobbin, docked next to his destroyer whose sailors began firing at the planes. In doing so, smashed all the bags of potatoes on the Worden. This is when the crew were throwing pieces of potatoes at the low flying machines. There wasn't anything else to throw at them as both of their guns were empty. All ammo was under lock and key. The next thing he remembers is that his ship headed for open waters to see if they could intercept a Japanese carrier but there were none in sight. He recalls feeling the heat of the Arizona. "We saw the Oklahoma roll over," he said. "The planes were so close that we could see the pilots looking down at us with a smirk on their faces." Alex felt pretty bad when the USS Worden was lost when she hit a reef near Attu, an island in the chain of the Aleutian Islands. They were a mile or so from the island's beach. He fought desperately to save his life in 28° water temperature. Today, the ship rests on the floor of the Bering Sea, taking with her the lives of 15 of his comrades.

In conclusion, I hope that in my short commentary on the Day of Infamy, I have not slighted any person or persons. Every serviceman about whom I spoke was indeed a valiant person. I personally wish to salute you and the city of Four Flags salutes you.

Gardens of Eden

The reason for my trip to Buffalo, New York this past summer was actually three-fold. The first and the second was to interview two octogenarians as both had stories to tell and thirdly and the most important of which was to attend their 62nd wedding anniversary. My wife accompanied me on this flight so we both benefited in so many memorable ways. Both of our friends had health problems but they so graciously obliged us with their past. Their very first meeting had to with music and dance and it wasn't too long after that the bells rang and shortly after that, they became dance instructors. This was in 1928. Last week, I told you about a lumber camp at MacDonald Rapids in Mackinac County. Today, we'll talk about Mrs. Mac from the gardens of Eden.

Our well dressed lady is the daughter of Italian immigrants from Calobria, Italy. Her father was Joseph and her mother was Josephine. Her parents came to America because of the rich and fertile lands in the state of New York. They were in this New World but a short time when the father met a tragic death at his place of work. Her mother remarried some time later and gave birth to seven additional children. One of which was Angela whose story you are about to hear.

She told me that her mother and step-father came to America on a cattle boat like so many other immigrants in the late 1800s and early 1900s. Her mother's second husband was, by chance, a very close friend back in Italy. I was rather fortunate to see this "worldly Eden". And now I know why Angela's father liked it here. It is one of New York's best produce territories. This is what he did in the Old Country, growing vegetables

When Angie's father arrived in New York, he bought a nine acre spread on which he built a house, barn, shed and made ready all that was needed to become a farmer. We drove to the old homestead, the house, the barn, the shed and the land that once produced an abundance of eatables. Being of Italian descent, she often gestured where she played as a little girl with her sister, walking, playing and working. She told us about the many times she walked to the woods, the orchard and the vineyard with her sisters where they would pick grapes, apples, walnuts, hickory and butternuts. She gave us a vivid description of the time her sister put on a pair of overalls and filled them with apples and as she neared the house, the bottom of the overalls gave way and all the apples rolled away.

I must tell you as we drove by Eden and all the other nearby towns, it reminded me so much of the small towns back home in Berrien County with its fruit belts. The only contrast was we saw acres of cauliflower, peas, corn, cabbage, lettuce and tomatoes. Angela told us about the vegetables that they grew on the farm and when they were brought to market. This happened in 1915 and today you will see them doing the same thing. The soil is so rich in Eden that there are second harvests. She told us about harvesting on their farm when they would leave the house at 4 a.m. to ride the fields in empty wagons. Around Eden today, you will see high powered tractors pulling tons of produce. She remembers seeing many women farmhands. New York's climate is quite similar to that of the Midwest as it does have unexpected frosts. Angela's father would often find frozen pea pods in the fields. Everybody worked hard even her mother when she said, "One season my mother picked peas off the vine while nursing her baby." Our senior citizen remembers the cabins having cook stoves for all the workers. "After working in the fields all day," she said, "we'd come home around 9 p.m. We often washed clothes on stones in the nearby creek. Just by listening to this lady, there were lessons to be learned. She pointed out the old barn and the driveway. She was so pleased, self-satisfied and happy about what she had back then.

The irrigation system in these parts was incredible and while we were there, it was at its peak performance. Evidently, the wells showed no signs of being exhausted. There were many streams in the vicinity that were also of great help. Why wouldn't there be enough water around here when there is a little town around the bend called Water Valley? The name, Eden, told me that everything that grew here was rich and plentiful like it was in the Garden of Eden!

The church that the family attended each Sunday is still located in this little hamlet and that's where Angela was baptized, received her First Holy Communion and was confirmed. The entire family usually traveled in an open wagon.

She recalls the day that her brother and sister saved her from drowning in a rain barrel. She walked to school every day at distance of one and a half miles. There were two rooms in the building. One took care of grades 1-5 and the other accommodated grades 6-12.

After a while, her father sold the farm and bought a small business something like a general store. It was after working in the store that the family moved to Buffalo and this is where those of Eden now live. The oldest of her kin is now in her 90s.

While we sat on the picnic grounds watching the young and the old celebrating the MacDonald's 62nd wedding anniversary, Angela turned to us and said with a grin, "Take a look over there, see all those playing volleyball? They're all mine except two." It usually takes a dozen players for the game but, believe me, there was a mob out there. You bet they were hers, her grandchildren and her great grandchildren!

Living together for three scores was not easy, nor will it be for anyone reaching that plateau. Indeed, there were many trying days to keep the knot tied. Not too long ago, I read some country news about an elderly lady who had one husband and advised, "Couples should have more commitment, more love, less talk about wanting to split up, and thankfulness for what God gives a person. Since this writing, we attended another wedding anniversary. A mere 50 years and it was really an inspiration to watch this couple walk down the aisle and to the altar and listen to their exchange of vows. We also watched the well-wishers as the couple returned. We do not see these occasions too often but when we do, it is something to behold. It is indeed a sublime moment.

At 82, this Italian lady still flirts about the dance floor as graceful as a butterfly. When she talks, her expressions are quick and gestured. Her hospitality is unmatched. She has never driven a car though she often directs traffic from the back seat. All in all, she is a joy to visit.

A Country Doctor

Crossing the Straits of Mackinac a few days ago was another thrill for me. I recall back in '57 when Big Mac was open for traffic for the first time. It was truly a wonder that most people thought would never be. It was obviously a miracle when the local Indians were looking at the superstructure and thought back a century or so when their ancestors canoed across these deep blue waters.

When I headed south through the top of Michigan's mitten, I didn't realize at the moment that my story in this week's column would begin at Petoskey. This was the birthplace of Dr. Fred E. Murphy, the father of Pat Murphy, one of Niles' dedicated educators.

I'm sure that many of our local people will certainly remember the geographical location in our story. Much of my account takes place in Leelanau County. One of Fred's first jobs was at the Round Oak in Dowagiac. He worked there for ten years. He then attended Wayne State University where he received his medical degree. He spent some hard years as an intern at the University of Michigan Hospital. After his internship, he began his arduous years as Leelanau's pioneer physicians. People here in Niles are still talking about Dr. Bonine and so it is with the folks of this northern region, that they still talk about Doc Murphy, their wonder man. I imagine the old timers still gather at the coffee shops, restaurants, street corners and at the local pubs, talking about how that young doctor fought the weather and superstition up and down the back roads and on the islands in the lake. They say that he was an institution. No one really knows how many thousands of babies he brought into the world in how many hundred snowbound farmhouses. We can't imagine how many operations he performed on people's kitchen tables by the light of the kerosene lamps. Some of his methods would probably not be popular in today's city hospitals. But the way he had to work wouldn't be popular either with most city doctors. Truly an example of a country doctor.

I personally would have been honored to have met this eminent man. As I am recording these beautiful memories, I have a feeling that "my cup shall runneth over" before I complete this narrative. Be that as it may, another week is coming.

This tireless man served at least ten towns in Leelanau County, towns such as Lake Leelanau, Empire, Northport, Maple City, Cedar, Isadore, Glen Arbor, Leeland, Suttons Bay and an Indian settlement by the name of Peshaby, the spelling of which is incorrect. On so many occasions especially during the winter months, he'd cover ten miles on snowshoes. His fee for house calls was 25¢ and for deliveries it would be $25 which also included prenatal care.

Pat tells me that he had a team of horses, Queen and Topsy, and they acted as "spares" when the father's Model T wasn't working. This great caring physician designed a snowmobile for that snow belt region. Up in Leelanau County, they have huge snowdrifts with the gales coming off Lake Michigan. I'm sure that our residents from that part of Michigan will attest to that. It was for this reason that Dr. Murphy made this contraption, known to him and to his friends as a snowmobile. I have the photo before me with its owner dressed up what appears to me as a bearcoat, standing, of course, beside it. Let me describe it for you. The two front wheels of the small car are removed from the machine and eight inch runners are installed in their stead. Two wheels on each side have been added in the rear, making it a total of six. Over these runs a steel tractor belt. The top speed of this marvel was 25 MPH and it would run five miles to a gallon of gas. Had it not been for this snowbank-buster, he never would have made all his calls.

The Murphy family had a cat named Tommy, weighing some 25 pounds and resembling a Canadian Lynx. They also had a dog named Pal who was spoiled rotten. He'd make his daily trips to the shopping center where his admirers would give him candy, ice cream and his favorite meats!! By the way, Tommy ended up with Arlene Dahl's grandmother.

Dr. Murphy was respected and loved by many in Leelanau County. Even the youngsters would often bring their dolls to be healed. He was strict and often demanded respect. Gardening was his hobby, if and when he had the time. People would pay him with vegetables if they did not have the money. So many times he would take money from his pocket and give it to Munson Hospital. People's debt to him ran in the thousands.

Back in the early 1900s, life was so different, so jovial, so make-shift. Those of us who lived in or around that era have so much to talk about. Just the other day I learned that in the old days, the dead were not embalmed. So in order to keep the body preserved, the person in charge would put a chunk of ice in a large tub and place it underneath the casket. All wakes were handled at the family home. A wreath would always be placed on the outside of the entrance door indicating that this was now the house of mourning.

The Murphys weren't exactly nomads but they did move around a bit from Petoskey to Lake Leelanau to Leland and to Cedar.

Besides the parents, the siblings included James, who was the oldest, then came Marcella, better known as Pat and the youngest was Helen. When they moved to Cedar, the town became a great lumbering center and today it has the distinction of having a sausage factory.

Dr. Murphy was often called to testify for crimes committed around the Traverse City area. No matter where he hung his hat, everyone invited him to stay overnight. Many people knew that he was a religious man, but not too many knew that he carried on his person the Rosary and each night before he retired, he would recite these beads. His family was indeed very proud of his faith. Being of such caliber, one would sometimes wonder, what manner of man was he?

The following message is a portion of a letter dated November 2, 1950 written by Dr. Coller and addressed to Mrs. Helen Timmerman, the daughter of Dr. Murphy: "Your father was a close friend of mine...I've known him for 30 years...he was a great physician, one who exemplified the highest ideals of our profession...his chief interest was always the health and welfare of patients which was untainted by commercial aspect. He and my father were the backbone of medicine." Dr. Frederick A. Coller was Professor and Chairman of Surgery from the University of Michigan Hospital.

Since he once was a resident of Dowagiac, the Murphy and Buckley families willed some property to the Sacred Heart Parish which is located off Downey Street. The Church today serves as a Mission to Holy Maternity Parish in Dowagiac. The Silver Creek Cemetery, which is just adjacent to this place of worship, has the names of the Murphy clan inscribed on several headstones. Pat tells me the names of her two uncles, namely, James and Daniel are clearly visible and so are the names of her two aunts, Mary Stahl and Anna Reagan. Those of you who enjoy browsing through graveyards, may I suggest that you visit Silver Creek as this one has the names of several Indians.

This healer of many in Leelanau County for 43 years died on December 1, 1948 at age 71. Both he and his wife, who passed away six years later, were buried at Traverse City.

The Murphys left a daughter, Pat, whom we have learned not only to love as a friend, but to respect her as being a permanent fixture in the Niles School System. She received her teaching degree from Kalamazoo Teachers College which today is universally known as Western Michigan University. Her first teaching assignment was in New Buffalo and then came to Niles in 1944 when Mr. Floyd Crawford was Superintendent and the irreplaceable Walter Zabel was Principal. These two administrators lived in the old Central School Building.

Pat speaks very highly of Ella Champion who was the Elementary Supervisor of the outlying elementary schools. She, too, was an institution ruling with an iron fist. Her philosophy and ethics were a credit to our community. Miss Champion was a dedicated teacher of 52 years. Besides her artistry, she wrote poetry which excelled in thought and beauty. One of her last paintings is now a Murphy treasure.

Going back to the top of Michigan's mitten again, let's follow the footsteps of this great man of medicine and find out some of the places he may have stopped with Queen and Topsy, his Model T, his snowmobile or just on foot.

I am sure that while you were at that small town of Cedar, you saw the sign that read Dr. F.E. Murphy, Physician and Surgeon.

There was a place in Leland that did some printing work making letter heads, bill cards and business cards. You were almost certain that Fred E. stopped there.

The bank at Cedar was destroyed by fire one year, I believe in the early 20s and if the doctor was in town then I am sure that he was one of the bystanders.

There have been times in his journeys that he parked to watch one of the steamers on Carp Lake between Leland and Fouch or he could very well have stopped to talk to a bunch of railroad workers who all looked as though they were ready for a "short one".

His tin lizzie always needed gas and you can bet that he filled her up at Van's Garage in Leland. Those of you who are from the Northport territory, do you remember the Wil

Johnson Store? It was a place known for its men's furnishings and groceries and kind of a meeting place for some folks.

I have no doubts about the doctor listening to some dandy fish stories coming from Lake Leelanau way. As I write you these lines, I have before me a photo of a man holding a musky which is almost as tall as he is! Come deer season, he undoubtedly heard their tales also.

Back in March 1919, there was a big train wreck at Suttons Bay which made much talk all over the County.

Gain's Barber Shop was located at Leland and I guess Fred made his occasional visits there. During the 30s and 40s, Dr. Murphy often stopped at the Mill Pond in Northrop to watch people skate. It's very possible that he stopped at Shalda's Grocery Store for a moment. At any rate, you were quite proud to hear about all those places from that scenic route in Michigan and you've boasted about it just as you have been hearing me speak in length about that great Land of Copper.

The Doorn Bunch

Some weeks have past since my spouse and I toured the Indian Lake territory. The sky was overcast that day and the temperatures were rather mild. I really wanted to see whether there were any die-hard ice fisherman from my vantage point. Instead, I caught a glimpse of something that brought back a thousand memories. It was hockey in the wide open spaces!

I had to go back about sixty-five years while living in the Copper Country, more precisely, in the village of Calumet. This is where the neighborhood gang would clear a section of the local dam to play hockey. Since this is the part of Michigan that has so many record snowfalls, we would spend hours in sub-zero temperatures getting our hockey rink in good shape.

Living in a melting pot of diverse cultures, the Slavs, the Germans, French, Italians and the Scandinavians, we learned so many things from each other and the one thing that I so vividly remember is watching the Swedes and Finns glide over the ice and show their skills with a hockey stick. This is when I became a novice of this great sport.

When I saw those young men chasing a puck, I couldn't help to bring to mind the many days we chased a puck and spent so much time looking for it in the snowbanks that outlined our playing field. After each game, around sundown, we would form a chain gang of buckets when it was time to flood our rink. Cutting a large hole in the ice would be our source of water. The way we chewed up the ice, we needed a new surface for our next skirmish. Even if we limped to the ice, the game would be on!

128

As I look back at my youth, I recall the days when I would make a small skating rink just adjacent to the old homestead. I would first pack the snow and then flood this area. Believe me, it took some patience but after a while, I had enough ice to learn how to cut corners, make a quick stop, skate backwards, and finally handle a hockey stick. All this while, I pictured my European neighbors doing the same thing in their backyards. I remember the first pair of skates that I owned. They were the type that were clamped on to the shoe or boot. Since they were my first, they became my most cherished silver blades. It was some time before I was able to buy a pair of tubular skates.

Skating and hockey became an obsession, not only for me, but for anyone living in that vicinity. Since winters were long and cold, we played ice hockey for many days, weeks and months.

There were many ponds in the area and when they froze over beginning in late October or early November, skating and hockey began in earnest and this would continue until March or April.

It seems that each day after school, I would round up the scrappers and after some years of this winter schedule, we became good skaters and stick handlers. We found our match though when we started competing with other locations.

Of course, I must tell you about our meager equipment. Our hockey sticks were the only earmarks of a hockey player. We played without shoulder pads and cups that were designed to protect the most vulnerable parts of our cold bodies.. We wore makeshift shin pads and I distinctly remember mine being thick magazines anchored by strips of old inner tubes from my father's Model T. Since goalie sticks were hard to come by, the goadltender used a small snow shovel. All of us wore ski caps and leather mitts. We played under these conditions for many years which, for some, left scars of hard play and moments of lasting exhilaration.

There are still a few of us left as friend and foe from yesteryear and if you were a passerby at our rendezvous, you will hear us say, "Remember when?" "Oh, yeah!"

I must also tell you that our life as an adolescent was not all fun and play but it was always work before we tied those skate shoe laces.

Now let's meet the bunch that gave me some beautiful moments to reminisce. When I returned a week later to this part of Indian Lake, I managed to corral a member of the ice gladiators on his way to their meeting place. He was the first of the Doorn clan that I met. His name is Cap. I joined up with him momentarily and this is when I met the rest of the Doorns pictured in the photo. This family has been cross-checking hockey sticks for a quarter of a century on different parts of the lake wherever the ice was suitable. It was obvious that they liked this sport so much so that they generated their own electricity for evening skirmishes.

Let's take a look and see who these people are. Pictured from left to right are Kip, Larry, Keith, Steve, Cap and Kevin. Those absent from this blood related group are Cal, Cory, Casey, Matt and Scott. Keith and Kevin are twins, whose brothers are Cory and Casey of which are the sons of the late Ron Doorn. I was told that at one time, that he too, was a hockey warrior. Cal, Larry and Cap are brothers and Scott and Matt are the sons of Cal. Steve is the son of Larry. All these names comprise the inseparable Doorn Bunch.

I don't know how many of you out there are aware of this amazing and unique family, but here they are all natives of Dowagiac and vicinity and are proud indeed to tell you that they are of Dutch descent. Little wonder then why they skate so well as their ancestors used to skate the Dutch Canals which were miles long!

I was fortunate to have met some of this bunch as they gave me something to write about - when all these years I thought that outdoor hockey was solely a sport played in the Copper Country!

Same blood, but different slapshots

Our Youth

If you've been feelin' kind of blue lately, maybe I can help to put a smile on your face. My story today will be all about you when you were a little girl. Whether you were a tomboy or just a plain petite and demure person. And you, sir, when you were just a kid, poor, rich or whatever. Perhaps the leader of the pack or one just being led. At any rate, I wish to talk about you, about all of us. Some of us are city slickers, just plain townspeople or maybe you lived in the country and I hope that you are not ashamed to tell our readers that you were raised on a farm.

It is so true that we all had a fling with some youthful activity or recreation. In my following thoughts, I am going to picture you in some situation in that place you called home.

If you came from the farm, we're watching you as you walked behind your father tending the plow being driven by his sturdy team of Belgian horses. One of your more pleasurable chores was going to the chicken coop to fetch some fresh eggs. You were so careful not to bother the hen, but it was just her nature to give you a peck on the hand. After the chores, you had some frisky moments in the front yard, running and chasing your brother and sister until you were all tuckered out. Those of you who had baby chicks sheltered behind the kitchen stove, watched your father or mother chopping up hard boiled eggs to feed the little ones.

It was a warm summer day when you and the gang sat on a fence chewing at a blade of grass wondering what to do next or you could have been just thinkin'.

I'm sure you have fond memories of running through some tall grass, much of which was overgrown buttercups that waved in the summer breeze. You were once told about the old fable that if anyone placed a buttercup under your chin and it showed yellow, you liked butter!

You also remember the old swing in your yard. The first one would always be a tire that your father tied to a big limb of a tree. Then a bit later, he made the real kind when a bunch of you kids tried to reach some low flying clouds. How about all the water pumps and buckets you'd see. Did you ever wonder why so many of today's greeting cards picture old barns and houses, pumps and buckets, barbed wire fences, old churches and schools? I'm sure that you recall your son or daughter and your grandchildren say to you, "Gee, it sure must have been nice back then!"

How many times have you looked at those musty books and photos, just lookin' and reminiscin'? I bet there must have been some heartbreakers in that pile. Just rummaging through all your stuff kind of touched your heart, didn't it?

The day that your daughter or grandchild picked you a bouquet of wild flowers, sneaked in the house, somehow and said to you, "Here." Don't you wish that was yesterday? And even if you were a man, and your own kin handed you a dandelion, wouldn't that be a tug at your heartstrings?

I saw a little boy clumsily wading through a puddle of rain water the other day and if that didn't ring a bell as it took me back a few scores when my mother scolded me for getting my shoes wet!

How many of our youthful games have changed in the course of time? Hide-and-go-seek is still around. How about hopscotch, jacks and marbles. I am sure there are many others. Even some that you made up yourself and handed down to the next generation and all their kids.

March winds brought you and all your friends out with your kites sending up signals up the string with cardboard disks. Can you remember making all these contraptions?

Aren't you glad that your father taught you how to saw and chop wood for the cold winter months ahead? He taught you how to use a sawhorse with a bucksaw or crosscut. Those of you who have never seen this operation haven't really lived.

Of course, there was always someone that was special to you. Someone with whom you exchanged glances. It was not that important, but still it was a beautiful encounter.

All those days you spent throwing, skimming and batting rocks into a big pond. Maybe this is why you became so fond of baseball.

Halloween was something special in your neighborhood. All of you used to go masquerading during your trick or treat runs. It was different than today as you didn't appear to be too demanding.

Your visits with your grandparents were moments that will live forever. Sunday came along and everybody went to church and you never asked, "Why".

I kind of think that your school days were rather special, too. You never had to worry about catching a bus and you very rarely complained about walking all that distance.

Then came Christmas and you'd always go to that certain spot to chop down the fir tree. Can you remember the times that you were in Christmas plays at school, singing carols and riding in horse drawn sleighs?

I sincerely hope that this little piece of writing still brings back beautiful memories of the good ol' days.

Tranquility

South of Dubuque, Iowa on Highway 151, beautifully and agriculturally nestled among the hills and dales, is a House of Prayer, Meditation and Contemplation. This is the house of the Trappist Monks. More specifically, New Melleray Abbey. It was founded in 1849 by the monks from Mount Melleray Abbey in Ireland. I am sure that most people of this city that borders the Mississippi River know about this Holy Place. However, most people in today's complex and troubled world are far removed from the cloistered life of a monk whose residence is called a Monastery. Both words are of Greek origin meaning solitude, solitary or a hermit. It is primarily a religious community. Hopefully, that this bit of research will help us better understand the lives and beliefs of these special people.

At this point, I would like to tell you about the early rise of this religious movement. Monasticism was practiced in Egypt around 300 A.D. People who chose this form of worship were called monks and, as a novice, he retired from worldly affairs, took the vow of poverty, chastity and obedience. While living in a monastery, he studied the scriptures, prayed daily, worked extensively in the fields and thoughts of God were his primary goals in life. Once he left the confines of the world, he devoted himself totally to God.

The life of a monk is austere indeed. You might say that it is somewhat beyond our comprehension as we just cannot realize why a man submits himself to a rigorous way of life to such solitude and simplicity. He has done this for countless centuries and will continue to do so. Different Orders of monastic life are universally located.

Perhaps the order of his day will give you some idea of what all is entailed in his life. To begin with, all monks are early risers and at daybreak, they are called by the sound of a small church bell reminding them to come to their chapel to pray. These morning prayers are referred to as Matins which are followed by the monk's participation in the Holy Sacrifice of the Mass. At its completion, they all retire for their morning meal. Soon after which they take part in their assigned work. Their next call for prayer takes place in the early hours of the afternoon. These readings are called Lauds. The final prayer at early evening are Vespers. All these prayers comprise the Divine Office which are Scripture Readings regulated by canonical hours (certain periods of day set aside for prayer). When a monk is not in prayer, he may either be asleep, eating his meager meal or working. Whatever the case may be, it is done in His honor.

The simple garb of a monk consists of a cassock (a long fitting garment) which is usually white in color covered by a black scapular hanging from the shoulders. The former of which has a cowl, (a hooded piece of cloth). Sandals are his daily footwear. A monk's place of sleep is rather crude, likewise his refectory (a dining hall in a religious house) each monk having a tin cup and plate.

Monastic life involves many bows of the head or body and genuflections (the bending of the knee). Upon the death of one of its members, the body is placed in a pine box with its head covered by the cowl. As time went on, it is possible that the burial ritual has changed. A private cemetery is still a part of every institution.

When all monks convene to pray, certain ones are chosen to be cantors as their prayers are chanted in the manner of Gregorian Chant which prior to the dictates of Vatican II, were sung in Latin. Today's devotions, however, are all chanted in the vernacular and at times harmonized.

In this community of the Religious, a monk is either a professed brother or priest, the young as well as the old. The latter is given more spiritual powers. Both professions accept identical vows.

In most cases, monasteries are located in rural areas just to be segregated from the cares and hustle and bustle of the world. These sacred institutions are self-sufficient as they have farms that produce hay, corn and soybeans along with milk from their own cows.

Prior to the 60s, silence was the absolute Golden Rule. There was only one selected from the cloistered, usually a brother, to answer the door. All others were subjected to the Rule. Even in recent times, silence is still quite the norm, for this enables them to be close to their Creator.

Today, there are many lay people that visit the Abbey. Some come out of curiosity still others come to enjoy a spiritual retreat (time spent for prayer and meditation). Many people take part in these spiritual exercises annually as this is a sure way of gaining moral fortitude.

In years past, my family and I have visited these hallowed grounds and have learned for the first time about its confines thereby being exposed to the rudiments of ancient history.

Since our children have grown and have gone their separate ways, my spouse and I have returned to this special place of tranquility. We often talk about this beautiful institution and about all its monks chanting their daily prayers. Just spending a few hours each day in this atmosphere of silence is worth its weight in gold.

Yesteryears

In order that I may free myself momentarily from the perplexities of politics, the current court proceedings and from so many other disturbing affairs, I would like to give an account of the events of many yesterdays. I am fortunate to have countless memories of my childhood, my adolescence and my years as a young adult.

Some weeks ago, I was inspired by a thought-provoking program that I had watched which impelled me to write this narrative about yesteryear. This gave me an opportunity to reminisce, to laugh and maybe even to cry. Here are some of those unforgettable memories. However, the events to follow will differ exceedingly from those of recent memory.

My travels and journeys were many in the course of time and on many occasions, I would invariably observe the Burma Shave signs that were installed along the straight and winding thoroughfares of our great nation.

The Fuller Brush man was a frequent visitor in our neighborhood and I'm sure he touched Timbucktu. As young as I was, I still remember shaking the hand of this global salesman. I was amazed to see his selection of brushes. It seems that everyone on our block bought a brush or two.

I truly relish the thought of waiting for the early milk delivery as this would be the opportune moment to lick the cream from the lid of the milk bottle. Today, I no longer hear the clippity-clop of the horse-drawn milk wagons.

World War II was in full swing over the Atlantic and Pacific Oceans. The home front, too, with its women of steel were making machines, airplanes, guns and ammunition for our fighting men in distant lands. I recall handling war ration stamps that were used to purchase gasoline or any item that was militarily controlled.

The little school house was indeed a learning institution and with it came discipline. The day started with a pledge of allegiance that was said with heart and soul. I often ran to school with both my lunch bucket and books dangling at my side. I took shortcuts through farmers' fields either crawling underneath barbed wire fences or jumping over tiny creeks and swales.

Perhaps my most exciting moments were the many days that I used to wait for the steam powered locomotive coming around the bend of the river. This big piece of machinery sped by the countryside leaving a trail of smoke that could be seen and smelled by the folks that lived along those sturdy railroad ties. I can still hear those train whistles that sounded in the wee hours of the morning. There were days when I'd edge my way through a crowded train depot just to watch people laughing, smiling, crying, hugging and kissing.

I was always impressed by the strong family ties that existed in our time. Everyone cared deeply for each other. Sunday picnics were the order of the day.

Although the Great Depression was a time of want, I did manage to get a couple of nickels and tear down to the local soda fountain for a double dip. I stayed there for a while and laugh and jabber with the rest of the bunch.

Was there anything more American than the brush of the artist, Norman Rockwell? His portrayal of man, race and religion was a classic and so was his scene of the country doctor. The Saturday Evening Post was the literary gem of the times.

Frequent bicycle rides to the old spring hole were refreshing for two reasons, first, the trip itself, and secondly, drinking ice cold water from the man-made bubbling fountain or cupping my hands to get a swallow from the tiny trickling stream below. And after this thorough enjoyment, I would haul some of this precious cargo home in a small pail which was to be readied for tomorrow's coffee pot.

In early spring, our family would frequently listen to the evening serenade of the croaking frogs and if this performance was short lived, then the lightening bugs would put on a spectacular show.

So much has escaped the American scene that, perhaps my interpretation of the past will bring to light the life of many yesterdays.

The General Store

I'd like to take you back several decades and show you a place that people often talk about today. This particular place has been portrayed in many television series' and whose stories are surprisingly enjoyed by the old as well as by the young.

Since I not only lived during the time of the General Store, I also lived by it and in it, so to speak. It was a spot of great camaraderie where people not only shopped for the necessities of life, but spent part of the day in idle talk. I treasured being here for the simple reason of listening to the old timers that would congregate around the potbelly stove exchanging stories about hunting and fishing about "the one that got away" and about the musky that shook the ice shanty when it was hooked. Stories about religion and politics were carefully discussed and sparingly I might add. For if pursued, someone's feathers would eventually be ruffled. And if all these conversations took place in the middle of winter, the coffee pot was always ready and waiting on top of the stove.

I had wished so many times that today's youth would have also shared what transpired in these houses of countless commodities. I am sure that they do have some knowledge of this past experience by watching various documentaries.

Now that I told you about some of the people that frequent these public places, may I tell you about the things that you are bound to see. The first time that I walked into one, I was absolutely amazed about the array of goods.

Once you set foot into this establishment, you wondered how a number of people could possibly have navigated in this cluttered structure even with all those big barrels lined up in the store. The kids enjoyed it though, as the owner saw to it that they would get a morsel of some sort of candy.

Yes, this store had just about everything. I would often see those sacks of flour. Homemade bread was a must back in those days. By the way, once those sacks were emptied, the material was used for dish towels.

Looking for breakfast cereal was no problem as your choice would be simple, Kellogg's Cornflakes, Wheaties or Quaker Oats. I just thought of an item that every home just had to have and that was a box or two of kitchen matches.

What store didn't display those huge pickle jars and a bite of one would almost be a meal. I'm willing to guess that the pickles were preserved by the local farmers. That's why they were so good.

I noticed on several occasions that mother would shop for gingham material. They also bought other material as they were all experienced seamstresses.

Directly in front of these stores were the gasoline pumps which were all manned by a side hand pump. You could always see the gas being pumped. You would always be well taken care of. When you left, your windshield was spotless.

During the summer months, people would often have sticky fly catchers suspended from the ceiling. Where would be the surest place to find these, the General Store, of course.

I remember the first time that I entered this building. It was about 10 a.m. when I was shocked to see an unusually large crowd assemble in and outside the store. I asked, "What's all the commotion?" They didn't hesitate to tell me that they were waiting for their mail. You see, Uncle Sam lived here, too.

I almost neglected to tell you that in the long narrow room was a butcher shop and I do mean an array of the finest cuts of meat.

Many patrons of this rural store would be especially pleased to know that they could purchase their goods on credit. I was told that they would be prompt with their monthly payments.

It seems that the folks in that era enjoyed reading the Farmer's Almanac. At one point, I became a self-taught meteorologist and knew something about horoscopic studies.

While I was writing this account, I thought of a man who was recently interviewed by Larry King. This man is America's Chairman of the Joint Chiefs of Staff, General John Shalilkashvili. What they talked about was so closely related to some accounts of my story. Mr. King asked the General, "What would you like to do when you retire?" And with a sheepish grin on his face, the General answered with a slight foreign accent, "I always wanted to be a clerk in a Hardware Store where I could use a ladder and reach for some nuts and bolts that a customer wanted." Can you imagine what he wouldn't do in a General Store?

One of the reasons why I took such great interest in telling you about these places of yesteryear is that I became well acquainted with the proprietor and his family. I learned so much from them not only about their livelihood, but mostly about their foreign heritage.

The Vanishing Red Barns

I remember while bicycling as a kid, I wouldn't miss seeing McClosky's big red barn. On one of its sides, there was a bold looking commercial that read "CHEW MAIL POUCH TOBACCO". Today, this barn stands no more and neither do so many others. If they are, they seem to be swallowed up by creeping and winding vines along with all the silos that hug these sturdy buildings.

While living in the uppermost part of the Upper Peninsula of Michigan, red barns were uncommon and I really didn't know too much about these mammoth structures. What this territory prided itself in, were the copper mining shafts that extended deep into the earth's belly.

And so when I moved to this land of much fruit and many red barns, our little family lived plumb next door to one of man's vanishing brands. This was a chance for the proprietor to show a greenhorn just how big this farming business was, growing acres of corn and milking a herd of cows. I do remember working on my uncle's farm but his spread couldn't come close to the farms in this area. I am grateful though, it taught me to appreciate the work of a farmer.

When I first saw these super structures, I was awed by the way they were built. I was truly fascinated by the long and strong timbers, especially the ceiling joists where I knew that at one time, every piece of wood had to be hewed perfectly.

There was a time when farmers took such great pride in looking at these structures. For the passers-by, it was truly a thing of beauty, and in recent memory, an ideal setting for an artist, as these wooden frameworks will in due time, become history. I was fortunate, indeed, to have been shown every nook and hook in this lofty home of domestic animals. It is very likely that most of today's generation will never see the exterior of the big red barn, much less its interior. It is for this reason, that I wish to share my experience with those who have never had the opportunity to know something about this famous country dwelling.

Come along now, and let's open the door and see for ourselves what really is in store for us. Many of these barns had a steel rod extended across the interior, for added support, I'm sure. In many instances, the farmer would install a heavy gauged rope on this rod which didn't have any function other than a swing for his children and their friends. Usually below this extension was a bed of hay which cushioned the fall of the acrobats. The hayloft was enormous and stored tons of straw and alfalfa.

The hogs had a special lodging which was just adjacent to the main premises. There were many bins that were used for storage of some kind other than grain. A bit further, we spotted a variety of shovels that hung from the siding along with long wooden rakes and pitchforks which were used for loading and unloading a hay wagon. This was the chore of an adult while the children packed the load in the loft and, believe me, this job was most exhausting.

Horses of a special breed were used for pulling heavy loads and plowing the acreage. These draft horses were kept in stalls which were outlined by several harnesses. Near the same area were chickens being watched by attractive looking Rhode Island Red roosters. The coop was busy with laying hens. In the early hours of each morning, I would see this same flock searching for tidbits in the farmer's yard.

This is the house of many cobwebs, bats, barn swallows, small screechy owls, birds, pigeons and hungry scurrying rodents. I am sure that we would see in the dark corners of the rafters spiders that were busy winding up their recent catch.

What barn doesn't have a concrete silo attached to one side where fodder was stored for a winter's supply of animal food?

The older barns all had windmills and when the wind was at top speed, there would always be enough water pumped into the watertank. This was a favorite stopping place for the cows coming from their pasture.

A ladder and kerosene lamp were permanent fixtures in every farmer's workshop. Upon careful observation, I could see spikes nailed to posts which were used for any conceivable farming equipment.

Since these barns harbored many animals, I noticed a wheelbarrow which was used to haul manure to a special area then thrown outdoors. This accumulation of animal waste was then used as rich fertilizer in the spring of the year.

Perhaps the most fascinating part of my telling you the story of red barns is the section where the cows, heifers and calves were located. It appeared that all milking cows were lead into stanchions during individual milking periods. Ten gallon milk cans were close by to empty the smaller pails of milk. The farmer always had company as he sat on a stool while milking as the barn's cats waited for a squirt or two.

Today, I picture the cows' pastures, the times the farmers lead them there and the times that he'd fetch them for milking. The cowbell was a beautiful sound especially if an animal was lost. With every herd throughout our dairy land, the farmer had his shepherd dog along to perhaps corral a stray or two or maybe just to keep him company.

Like the ancient walls of Rome and Greece, the old red barns have reached their time to crumble and with each collapse, also go a thousand memories. We can truly say that they have aged gracefully and the elements of nature have finally taken their toll.

Bishop Frederick Baraga

This is a story about a snowshoe priest, Frederick Baraga, who followed the footsteps of other trail blazers, namely, Fathers Marquette and Allouez. Some 200 years after these Jesuits battled the wilds of the forest and the wild attitudes of the Indians, this newly ordained cleric came to America from Slovenia, one of the Republics of Yugoslavia. It was his ardent desire to continue the ways of Christianity.

After Baraga's short stays in Cincinnati, Detroit, Grand River, and places along the western shores of Lake Superior, he chose to remain with the Chippewas and Ottawas on the eastern shores of this Great Lake as well as the northern section of Lake Huron.

In the course of my extensive travels throughout the Upper Peninsula, many people had told me stories about this missionary. Since I personally had seen areas where this man of God worked, I would like to take this occasion to tell my readers about some of the Indians to whom I spoke, whose ancestors walked and talked with this Blackrobe.

The snowshoe priest's evangelization of these Indian tribes started around 1833. Everyone knew that this man walked many miles each day to take care of the spiritual needs of the red men. All his winter travels were on snowshoes and many of his journeys were also by portage.

Father Baraga was quite amazed about the way the Indians made their canoes. He often watched them rip large strips of bark from birch trees. These pieces would then be sewed together and fastened around the framework of spruce wood. The bark had to be moist and all the seams were filled with melted pitch.

The young missionary was quite anxious to have his first ride in a canoe which eventually helped him to reach far off places. As I write these lines, I picture him accompanied by two young braves plying their new canoe across the choppy waters of a lake. The places that he visited were scattered throughout the U.P.

At all times, you would see this blackrobe clad in his cassock which was the traditional garb of all clerics. He also wore a pectoral cross which I am sure that he used to show and bless his flock. When he finally settled in the north country, many people would ask, "Where does he really live?" He must have had some headquarters, but his home was everywhere. Being on foot so many times, he undoubtedly would bunk under some make-shift lean-to. This was another lesson the Indians gave him. And since his friends were great trappers, many of their pelts were not only used for warmth but the hides were used for snowshoes which in time were his surest means of winter travel. Story has it that as Baraga was nearing the home of a shut-in, he suddenly collapsed in the snow with his snowshoes still strapped to his feet. It wasn't too long after that, that he regained his strength. It was through sheer exhaustion that his journey ended so abruptly.

Living with and administering to the Chippewas and Ottawas, this European cleric began to know the language of these people so well that he composed an Indian Dictionary. Besides his native Slovenian tongue, he had to master the English and since he became such a close friend of the Indians and because of his daily visits with the North American Indians, he soon knew the letters, the words and the sounds of this strange language.

I picture this snowshoe priest as being tall and lanky rather raw boned and his brownish long hair parted in the center. His face always appeared to be weather-beaten which surely gave evidence that he spent countless hours in the heat of the sun or facing the chilled northerly winds. He was often seen wearing a round black brimmed hat which he also wore in winter with some make-shift earmuffs.

Henry Wadsworth Longfellow, America's most influential poet, lived in the same era as our evangelist and in his poem "The Song of Hiawatha", he wrote about the Chippewas.

Being surrounded by virgin timber, this ambitious blackrobed missionary worked hard building little log chapels. His catechumen braves would help him with these tiny places of worship. Since his young assistants were also skilled hunters with their bows and arrows and clever with their fly fishing, there was always much meat and fish on the table.

Because of his untiring efforts and saintly work, Frederick Baraga was chosen by the Holy See to be the first bishop of Sault Saint Marie which later became the Diocese of Marquette in 1857. The mission of Bishop Baraga, the snowshoe priest, was completed in 1868.

Sandwiched in the Bay of Keweenaw, a natural harbor of the Great Lake Superior, stand the little towns of L'Anse and Baraga. This was once the great fishing grounds of the Chippewas and Ottawas. They liked what they saw and heard and so they named this place of many canoes, Baraga, after their great Spiritual leader.

Symbol of sovereignty

149

Bishop Barga & Guide

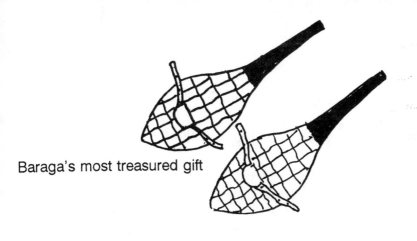

Baraga's most treasured gift

Snowshoe imprints
in front of St. Mary's Church
Soo, Mi

151

The Land of the Eagle

There is no more distinguished symbol of our beloved country than the bald eagle. It symbolizes strength, supervision and vigilance. It makes its daily tours combing the beaches of the northern Great Lakes and scans the heavy terrain of the Upper Peninsula of Michigan. Its habitat really is everywhere in this rugged country. Its nesting place is located in the towering pines and hemlocks bordering the many lakes of this great state.

I have seen this beautiful bird on many occasions during my excursions throughout this wild country. It has fascinated me to see it soar above the calm and stormy waters of Lakes Superior, Michigan and Huron. I have often wished that I could better visualize the majestic wilderness of this peninsula as that seen from the eyes of the eagle. It is with this thought in mind that I write about my travels, my episodes and my adventures in an area that is predominately besieged by a diversity of trees, lakes, ponds, rivers, creeks and streams, the swails, knolls, and countless hills.

While on these tours in nature's panorama, I was simply awed by the presence of innumerable deciduous and coniferous trees. Many were flanked by rippled ponds, meandering creeks and mosquito-ridden marshes while other just stood there stately spiraling toward the sky like launch pads. There were hemlocks lofting about weathering the storms like Gothic cathedrals. Not too distant were groves of aspens whose leaves seem to twinkle with each gentle breeze. Over the next knoll were the aging and scarred pines showing another passerby some ideal compass point. Close-by were their relatives, the dark and shady spruce hugging the floor of this dense forest. Below the ridge, were the obnoxious tag-alders screening the treasured beaver ponds teeming with scrappy brook trout.

I stopped for a moment to watch mosquitoes caught in a tree-hung spider web while feeling a gentle breeze scented with new-born leaves. I stood in the midst of a cluster of ferns just spewed from the earth.

My hatchet blazed a trail to a recently discovered trout stream. About me, I could smell decayed wood and early arbutus. I could see stumps ravaged by Michigan's black bear which appeared like remnants of a tornado. I found myself standing in a land that harbored the untamed and untamable.

As I made my fly casts, I could hear the trickle of a beaver dam. It was just a matter of minutes before I reached the engineering feat of this ruddered creature. I splashed clumsily in its canals and couldn't help but observe the beauty and stillness of this pond. I caught a glimpse of his secluded lodge made from alders, chips and chewed saplings. For the first time, I saw this master at work and showing off his supremacy. His sudden splash startled me but this was his way of showing his kits the early trade of navigation. The view was unbelievably beautiful and the trout were in abundance.

Evening in the wilds is spine chilling when you hear the howls of the coyotes and the rummaging of bears. I would often whistle in the wilderness just to calm my edgy nerves. The sounds, sights and smells of this desolate land are many and varied. As I walked on an old tote road, I heard the croaking frogs serenading the blues of the night in the nearby slews. Across the marsh, the eagle's cousin, the hawk, was perched on a dead tamarack screeching over his domain like a commanding sentry. Just below his view, was a drumming partridge whose sound would mystify a novice of the forest. I realized then that I was in a place of the nocturnal kingdom and I wondered just how many of these being crossed my path and how many saw me from their crouched position. There must be a thousand ears in the forest as animals steal their way along fixed and make-shift trails. The song of the vesper sparrow comforts my thoughts of being alone. Not too far, were the roaring falls and burbling rapids of another trout stream. At evening's rest, I was pleased to hear the wavelets that lapped against the beach near my campsite yet somewhat stirred by the wild cries of loons on this foggy lake.

There's no question that my journeys in the forest became an obsession with every observation, noise and trace of all animate and inanimate objects. I often wondered about the countless pools in shaded ravines and about the miles of knolls and swails that showed signs of buck rubs and deer runways. I was so struck by the huge ridges that made me feel as though I were in the belly of the earth.

I enjoyed the smell of mushrooms and morels hiding in the damp earth, rotting leaves and pine needles. The smell of rotten timbers gave evidence of being riddled by drilling woodpeckers. It was rather obvious that this was the advent of another season.

I was absolutely amazed to watch the flights of Canadian Honkers making their way south. Amazing, too, was the quartet of mallards shoveling and shuffling for algae while nearby their ducklings copied a new pattern of life. It was then, too, that a dawn patrol of canvasbacks made a perfect landing just beyond the reach of my 16 gauge.

While standing in the brush, there were tiny pesky gnats resembling dancing atoms, determined to make my presence miserable. I managed to use every means possible such as a branch or fern to avoid their sting. I chanced upon a colony of ants; armies of carpenters and harvesters making tree canals, storing food, invading and pillaging enemy territory. At twilight, there were lightening bugs that resembled distant flashlights. I recall the countless moments when I plowed through spider webs with a feeling that I was being entangled in a fine mesh.

From the eagle's vantage point, the forest is a castle of solemnity, sublimity and sovereignty. It is the place that keeps the eaters and the eaten. It is the home of the fleeting deer, the howling wolf and coyote, the cunning fox and wildcat, the ever varied snowshoe hare and his enemy, the weasel, and the biggest of all, the black bear. All living beings in this vast land are enchanted by the sun, the moon, stars, rain, snow, wind and sky.

I recall my first hike to a far-off dilapidated lumber camp once owned by Bushnell in Keweenaw County in the vicinity of Bete Grise. This is where, for the first time in my life, I lived and slept under the stars and heard new sounds that have since then captivated me. In the camping party, there were youngsters, my father and my uncles Tony and Frank. Listening to these adults telling us some hair-raising stories was quite an ordeal especially when it was time to get some shut-eye for those two nights. We came to this remote area, not only to enjoy camping under a lean-to but also to fish Copper Creek which flowed just below our confines. Having trout for breakfast and snacks are moments that will permanently enrich the memories of those who still survive.

Blazing trails at my fishing and deer hunting grounds almost became a ritual but it did save me many steps and continuous wandering. After a quarter of a century, I can still see outlines of the marks made by my hatchet. Since then, many waters have flowed under bridges and my places are still frequented producing much joy and indelible memories. It could be said that the eagle surveyed this place, too.

The days of the Great Depression have left us with CCC roads which have become the annual routes of the hunter and fisherman. While driving on one such route, I had the occasion to witness the fight of two partridges and further down the road, I was amazed to see another of the eagle's

155

cousins swoop down and snatch a snowshoe hare and disappear into the pines. There was so much to be seen while en route.

The streams, rivers and creeks that enticed me the most are all located in the Upper Peninsula starting at the very top is the Black River and Brewery Creek in Hougton County and in Keweenaw County, there is the Silver, Montreal Meadows, the Montreal and the ever popular and infamous Garden Brook! In Gogebic County, there is the Presque Isle River and in Alger County, there is the Scotts, Slapneck and Prarie Creeks and finally in Mackinac County, there is Taylor Creek, the Carp and Little Brevort Rivers. In recent years, camping at the waters of the latter two has given me immeasurable satisfaction. In my countless days of travel on the CCC Roads in Mackinac County, I witnessed something late one summer that I have never seen or heard about before. While camping with my son, we saw a pick up truck dragging a large pine tree over these sandy roads and wondered, why? The next morning, we spotted two hikers with walkie-talkies closely checking the road and it was at this time that we learned about the tree drag. They told us that they were covering all the old tracks of animals that may have crossed the road during the day. Since they were training their dogs to track bear, they were searching for new tracks. It was obvious that the older of the two men with whom we spoke was well versed in tracking various animals.

It wasn't long ago that my son, my brother and I drove through Iron City Trail headed toward the banks of the Montreal River located in the vicinity of Lake Medora (Mosquito). This was real rugged country most ideal for beaver ponds. We were lucky to have an overcast sky as this was the kind of sky that the trout wanted. I stood on the edge of a small dam and noticed an elevated terrain just ahead of me. It was another dam and just above that, there was another and another and finally, another. All were perfectly constructed and engineered by a beaver family. Our campsite for the day was located just a stone's throw from this ingenious design. It was truly something to behold. I must tell you that our limit of trout was well prepared in the skillet over an open fire.

Shuffling through the leaves of autumn brings back memories that are worth their weight in gold. Their shape, their smell and texture have affected me during my adolescent years. It was also during this time in my life that I learned why I was asked to gather leaves in a gunnysack and empty them in small storage bins which were prepared for garden produce. Winters were long and hard and fresh vegetables taken from the bins was indeed a welcome sight. Since the trees were now barren, there would always be, clearly visible, some large feathered predator perched on the tallest limb watching my every move. As we are all so well aware that the eagle's best vantage point is the highest and the most towering resting place.

Naturally, there are many untold stories about the wilderness and before the one that I am about to record becomes oblivious, I would like to shed some light on something that happened during a deer hunting season. There was an unusually mild November back in the 50s to do any serious deer hunting. It was most ideal, though, to live in a tent and sit outside on some makeshift stool eating your simple meal. We didn't have any Chef's salad, but what we did have sure stuck to our bellies.

I didn't join the hunting party at the onset so later that day, I was rather curious about their first day's hunt. "Did you get any?" I asked. One of them blared out and said, "Yeah, we got two Bucks!" They told me about this at the country pub where spirits of all sorts were high. We were about five miles from camp four by car and a mile on foot. Our special camaraderie broke up around midnight so we headed toward the rendezvous with the wilds. There was a chill in the air that night. We wondered why one or our party of four stayed some distance behind. The darkness was unbelievably thick. I did worry a bit, but was promptly consoled by one of the others. It was quite late when we reached our bunkhouse and you might have guessed that I wanted to see those two Bucks. "All right, where are they?" I yelled. Just then, I heard a chuckle from the one who brought up the rear. The other two took me down a small path with their flashlights and pointed to a limb of a huge fir tree. "Where?" I asked. "Right in there!" they pointed again. They spread the limb a bit and said, "There!" This was a sight that I shall remember all my life. There were two "bucks" all right, two U.S. dollars pinned to the tree. This is when the instigator stepped in and broke into a roar and so did the other two. It took us quite a while to fall asleep.

There are just two of us now to tell you this story. A brother and brother-in-law have now reached their eternal rewards. Another brother and I still have occasions to reminisce. All these hilarious moments took place in Houghton County beginning at Twin Lakes Rendezvous continuing on to a small spur at Winona and ending up at Stratton lumber camp.

While I am on the subject of comedy, there was another event that had happened several years prior to the same area. There were several people involved in an old lumber camp. They staged a brawl intended for one of their comrades. It lasted for some time, I was told, and it did bother the one for whom it was intended.

These are just some of the memorable events that tool place in the land of the eagle.

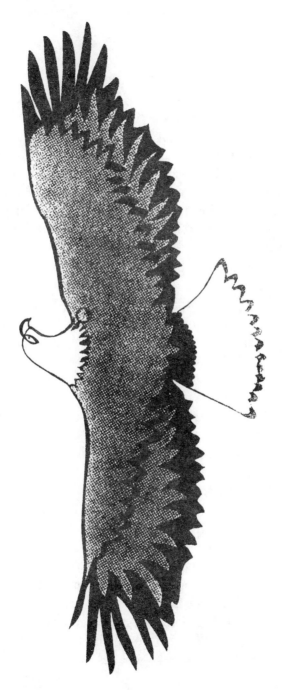

Soaring over his domain

Trout Obsession

Let's start from the top of Michigan, a piece of land called Calumet. Today, it is merely a tiny village that carries countless memories of a copper boom town dating back to the early 1900s. This was a time in American history when thousands of immigrants came to the New World to find prosperity and freedom. Many of these people came to Calumet where copper was king and employment was quick and plentiful.

In this group of early settlers were the Finns, Scandinavians, Poles, Croatians, Slovenes, Italians, French, German and the Cornish from Cornwall, England. I am an offspring of Croatian immigrants and raised in proximity of the ways of other European cultures. I am sure that it was the peoples of Northern Europe who showed me the ways of northern exposure. Fishing was their forte and so it was that I, in time, became a true disciple of the outdoors.

I must go back and tell you about events when I was just a kid playing baseball in open fields, crazy about trout fishing, playing hockey on frozen ponds, busying myself with many chores and having good clean fun. I used to watch my father coming home from a day's hunt or just roaming the woods. His clothes always smelled of the forest. I often sat and listened to him in his foreign language telling me about small game hunting such as the snowshoe rabbit and ruffed grouse. It was he who told me about the drumming of the partridge which, to me, sounded like an Indian powwow. I believe that big game hunting was his favorite.

I just remembered a large framed picture of my father taken around 1905. He posed for this photo sporting a handlebar mustache, holding his prize 12 gauge shotgun and strapped to his belt was a brown snowshoe rabbit. Sitting beside him was his irreplaceable hound dog. My sister is the proud owner of this masterpiece and maybe, in time, it will grace the confines of my living room.

Food on our table was good and plentiful. Meat from the wilds, dairy products from Bossie, the cow, and poultry products from the Rhode Island Reds that my father tended. We lived during the Big One, the Depression that is, and my father provided meat for the table by hunting wild game. My mother would preserve the wild meat in glass quart jars sealed with a wire fastener.

There was always some form of fresh produce prepared after the fall harvest. It was my job to pick wild strawberries, raspberries, thimbleberries and blueberries. These, in turn, would be made into jams or jellies, a winter treat especially on homemade bread.

It was at these berry patches, I believe, that a certain obsession was beginning to form. There was a little stream in the area that caught my fancy. The brook being fresh, my friends would always tell me that these kinds of waters had trout. Since my father often talked about the forest, its trees, the ferns, the mushrooms, the mosses and the many windfalls, I naturally longed to see and be with all these things. I knew, too, that somewhere in these surroundings, there would be inviting trout waters. Such was the case in every adventure.

I was about seven or eight when, for the first time, I walked to a tiny creek located a few miles from my home. It was in the area where I had found most of my berries. The place I had fished was just a spring hole that gave me many years of pure delight. During this era of great want, fishing poles were hard to come by so when we did reach our fishing spot, we'd cut a branch from one of the nearby tag alders and attach our fishing line. These we called "government poles" a name given perhaps because they were taken from State or Federal property.

This little stream was a feeder to Brewery Creek which meandered down to Lake Superior. I am convinced that it was this particular landscape that started my obsession for trout fishing. In recent years, I have visited the grounds of my childhood but the terrain has overgrown so much that one would have to crawl to reach the stream. I have now just passed the septuagenarian mark and, if I were able, I could take you to the exact spot of my early expeditions.

A moment ago, I told you that we always had meat on the table and I must tell you that fresh brook trout, too, was there for an appetizer!

On my many trips to this trout-spectacular, I had an ingenious plan to put some live fish in a bucket of water and take them home and place them in a large wooden clothes tub that my mother discarded. I would then fill the tub with freshly pumped spring water. In the tub, I also put a small hallow stump which served as a natural habitat for my smuggled trout. Since we did not have any running water, I would change the water frequently. I remember on one hot summer day when I checked my aquarium and I was startled to see two dead fish outside the tub. For a moment, I thought that there was some foul play, but then realized that trout like to jump for flies. Maybe it was this discovery that impelled me to take up the art of fly fishing later in my life.

For many years, I used live bait for fishing. There were times that I would sneak to the water's edge and drop my line into the slow moving current that disappeared a short distance under the bank. A sudden catch would move me. I wonder how many of you out there have experienced the same.

I enjoyed this sport beyond words. I would often take along some lunch as I would "make it a day". By the time I returned home with my usual mess of trout, I was bushed.

The first place I hit when I did get home was Ma's pantry where I had a piece of that delicious oven-baked bread spread with some homemade jellies. What memories!

Funny thing, but I was the only trout nut living in our vicinity. Why others didn't take to this sort of outing kind of baffled me but then, on second thought, none of their fathers enjoyed the outdoors. I find this to be a good time for character molding and I encourage others to follow suit.

My wardrobe for these exciting outdoor events was an old pair of tennis shoes used to walk in mud and in water and without fail, I wore a pair of overalls which gave me ample room for my fishing gear which, of course, included some form of fly dope. Oh yes, what would I do without my Prince Albert can filled with worms? There was a place for that, too. I always took along a small canvas bag that hung in our porch and when I reached the stream, I filled it with fresh leaves and ferns to keep the trout firm.

My parents always wore a big grin on their faces each time I walked into the kitchen with my canvas bag and gently threw my catch in the sink. It was my chore, by the way, to clean these beauties. I remember pumping cold water on them just to make them look fresher. This naturally pleased my father that I, the youngest of the family tree, would also make his own path through the wonders of nature.

There was a small unnamed creek that flowed underneath a road that ran by my uncle's farm at Phoenix in Keweenaw County. Our family would visit them frequently during the summer months. This was my time to nail that tiny body of water. This was another one of those spring-fed holes where I would practically tiptoe to drop my line. Believe me, all my tiptoes paid dividends.

I learned so many things about the night sounds of the forest. I recall the sound of an osprey as it perched on a towering hemlock overlooking my special trout stand. This, too, was his territory and it showed me its displeasure.

Usually at twilight when I stood near the shore of an inland lake, I would be alarmed by the loud screams and echoes of loons patrolling some remote area of the lake. As the sun was sinking in the west, the eerie hoots of owls would put a chill up and down my spine. Just then, two or more coyotes would fill the air with their scary ahhhhooooooo!

The sound that once baffled me while camping by a beaver pond was a terrific splash during the night. I do remember saying, "What was that?" The adults in the camp told me that it was the tail of the beaver hitting the water.

My first big venture into the camping world was perhaps in the late 20s. This was my initial step in learning how to rough it. I was pretty excited to know that we were going to spend the night under the stars, a little scary, though because I was a novice at this sort of thing. We were headed for the eastern shores of Lake Superior, more specifically, the area near Lac La Belle and Bete Grise. Evidently, my father had heard about this territory from some of his hunting companions and that it was an ideal spot for brook trout. That was enough for my ears!

Our itinerary read Copper Creek, a place where the lumberjacks of Bushnell's Camp worked and lived during the winter months. After we unloaded all the camping paraphernalia from our Tin Lizzies, we started our trek on one of the old trails that led to the abandoned camp sites. It was roughly a three-mile hike through an overgrown path, at times showing little signs of early travel. Some of the outstanding points of this expedition were small spring-fed streams that crossed this primitive road. There was only one way to find out whether these tiny tributaries had any trout and that was to try them. This we did and with whopping success. These trout were especially beautiful as they were brilliantly colored. Indeed, they were pure native trout. There were three or four such brooks trickling down to some inland lake, or better still, down to Copper Creek.

We had a shepherd pup that tagged along, frisky as any pup would be, until it managed to find a live trap set by some trapper. I watched the older members of the camp tackle the job of releasing the animal by placing a stick in the dog's mouth while someone else opened the trap. While on the move, I remember seeing Breakfast Lake and the mountains Houghton and Bohemia. I learned sometime later that these places became privately owned fisheries being that they were in the proximity of Lake Superior.

When we arrived at our campsite, there was just an outline of a lumber camp with the evidence of two dilapidated walls and overgrown weeds. This was to be our home for the night. Since this was to be my first ever under the galaxies, this was also a time for the older people for spoofs and spooks.

Since my father was the engineer of the forest, an open fire was in the making which meant that all of us had to gather some pine boughs and ferns for our bedding. You might have guessed that all this while, too, that Copper Creek was just a stone's throw from our lean-to's. I could hear its babbling and pictured scrappy trout lurking above the rocky floor.

Once the fire had a good start, we all sat by it and talked about all the things we saw and did on our way to the home of the early lumberjacks. It was time now for a good night's rest at least for those who could sleep. I'll tell you one thing, daybreak was not soon enough.. I was the first to tear down this embarkment rushing through some tall thistles and grass that was heavy with the morning dew. Was this an obsession? I am able to conclude this portion of my story by telling you that this was indeed a trout bonanza!

Some years later, by brother and I blazed a trail to Silver River whose headwaters are located a short distance behind the village of Ahmeek and its mouth being Lake Superior. It was at this stream that I witnessed some of the cares of nature. While fishing from a dingy, we spotted a mother beaver with her kits swimming just ahead of us in a V shape. We came too close for their comfort and each dove for cover, splashing their tails, of course. This was truly a sight to behold.

Perhaps the longest and best trout stream in Keweenaw County is the Montreal River whose headwaters are at Central Mine and its mouth would be the Big Spring, namely, Lake Superior.

I believe the notable sound of the vesper sparrow brings to light my next brush with the wonders of nature. The name Montreal Meadows has always been held in high esteem in my fishing book of memoirs. I have fished these meadows for many years not only for its serenity and productive waters, but also for the classic tones of the vesper sparrow.

It was back in 1948 that I had an occasion to fish the South Branch of the Presque Isle River in Gogebic County. Incidentally, this was my last outing with live bait. Stub Reid, the trout buff from Ironwood, Michigan, took me along for some fly rod action. Getting to the stream was a little difficult as we had to cross the Wisconsin border through some muddy ruts and back again to Michigan. Stub posted me by an eddy with which he was familiar and he walked down further, undoubtedly, to one his favorite spots. You might have guessed that I was plunking with my live bait for quite a while. I thought I didn't do too badly until the master fly fisherman came by. As a matter of fact, I heard him coming through the brush and, with his guttural voice, yelled out, "How ya' doin', Ed?" I showed him my reel and he gave me a compliment, "Not bad." He continued, "Here, let me try." I should have known that he obviously knew every bend in that river and this eddy was no exception. Directly across from my stance was a tiny feeder stream which I was not aware of. That was his target and let me tell you something, pardner, I was absolutely stunned to see the action of his rod and its results. Stub had a big grin and said, "Not bad, huh?" Not only did this guy know how to catch trout, but he tied his own flies. He told me afterwards that if I really wanted to know what the fish were taking, hook one first, open it and check its stomach.

The next day, I invested in a fly rod and started practicing in my back yard. I even began tying my own flies and what a thrill it was to latch on to a trout knowing that it was my fly that fooled him!

It is not unusual for a fly fisherman to find it difficult to fish a trout stream that is partially covered by a heavy growth of alders, cedars and another nemesis, the windfalls. Those of you who are diehard trout fisherman know that this is not a place for one with a fly rod, but it is for one who can crawl and withstand the thick brush and even, on occasion, step on a hornet's nest. Should this happen, then what?

In the past when scouting a trout stream, I listened for rapids or the sound of small falls which would tell me that a dam was around the bend. This has happened to me many times. Once I found this to be true, I made my cautious approach, a move that would remind one that the enemy lies ahead! Waiting for that ripple has paid off a hundredfold.

If I may, at this point, give you a reason why I would choose fly fishing in preference to bait, it is simply the excitement when the fly hits the water and the fish makes that sudden roll. For me, this becomes an obsession.

Let me take you to Mackinac County back in the 50s when I lumbered into some heavy beaver country. Some of the natives of this territory told me about beaver cuttings that they had seen that spring. And this is how I chanced upon a beaver at work. I was on top of a ridge when I spotted a large black animal and, naturally, it frightened me as it brought back that incident at Garden Brook. Since this sight was so spectacular, I just sat there and admired another wonder of nature. I learned then how this engineer builds his dams and how well he takes care of them. There was enough time to go down and try his new dam and get a few lunkers on my newly made wet fly. This was Silver River country.

Besides wading the Montreal River, I often fished the Meadows which were the most ideal for fly casting. Not only because of the open country, but also because of its fighting browns.

Since I lived in Mackinac County in the 50s and early 60s, I found a stream off one of the roads that the CCCs built during FDRs era. To this day, it has been kind of a haven for me and my family. Truly a retreat from the humdrum of modern technology and city madness. We find so much room to camp, to explore and just to look at the brilliance of nature. And, of course, my fly rod is there and I wait for the song of the vesper sparrow.

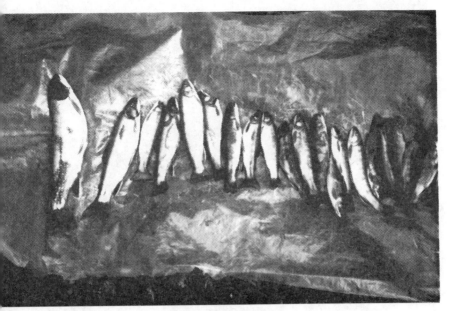

Trout bonanza!

The forest engineer's domain

Takin' a five

Michigan, A Land of Rich History

Mike Cain, our town's courier, invited me to sit in at a recent Historical Society meeting. He told me that Wayne Stiles, the Saint Joseph Museum Director, would be the guest speaker. I didn't hesitate to go as I knew that we would be in for a treat. Wayne's talk was all about Fort St. Joseph and if you forgot to attend, you missed a very prolific evening.

It was really through Mr. Stiles' presentation that gave me the impetus to tell you something about Michigan's larger forts. We will start from the very top of our state where the snows come early and stay late, down to the deep and swift currents of Lake Michigan and Huron, and continue on to the southwestern part where we will be sloshing through the swamps and meadows that lead to Fort St. Joseph.

At the top of Keweenaw Peninsula, back in 1844, the copper miners were fearful of an Indian uprising. This land belonged to the Chippewas. The workers had asked the Secretary of War, William Wilkens, to have a fort built in this area. It wasn't too long after this request that a fort was built and named after William Wilkens.

My father, who was an avid outdoorsman, often spoke of Fort Wilkens and I remember as a young boy, I would brush my fingers along the poles that surrounded the post. It was some years later that I had the occasion to go inside the premises and inspect some military artifacts and things essential to everyday living. My family would make several trips to this part of Keweenaw where we would camp, fish and pick blueberries. The specific place was Horseshoe Harbor which was a short distance from the Fort. These are events and places that are most outstanding in my childhood. I also

171

remember my father telling me that there was an old military trail used by the soldiers. The road ran from Copper Harbor to Eagle Harbor, a distance of 14 miles or so. This undoubtedly was their training area. Since this was the land of much copper, it was in this vicinity that this metal was mined and sent to the south to be used by the militia of the Civil War. Iron ore, which was mined in Gogebic and Marquette Counties, was also sent and used for warfare.

Fort Wilkens never experienced any hostility and during the WPA days, it was restored to its original state, and is surrounded by several lakes, first and foremost by Lake Superior and followed by the inland lakes of Fanny Hooe, Bailey and Manganese all of which made an ideal situation for Indian attack.

For those of us who enjoy reading Michigan history, it might interest you to know that Isle Royale, an island in Lake Superior, also a part of Keweenaw County and now a National Park, was once inhabited by the prehistoric Indian. Historians tell us that they were our first copper miners. You perhaps have wondered how the Chippewas came to settle in Upper Michigan. Perhaps they were the descendents of the early Indian on the Island. Since this strip of land was too distant to travel by canoe to Keweenaw, these tribes could have chosen to canoe along the northern shores of the Great Lake. Once they crossed the St. Mary's River at Sault Ste. Marie, they continued west along the southern shores and eventually landing at the Keweenaw Peninsula. This maneuver unquestionably took hundreds of years. Whatever route they chose, the Chippewas were the first to have squatter's rights and after some short negotiations, they ceded their rich copper veins to the U.S. Government. If we were watching and listening to all that was going on at this small northern stronghold, we knew that it became a friendly atmosphere with every soldier now standing at ease.

But as we traveled south along Lake Michigan, where it meets Lake Huron, we were beginning to hear war drums. We were now standing in hostile country which was a big piece of land harboring many Indian tribes including the Iroquois, the most warlike and fearful of all.

When the bands of Indians came with their canoes, they spotted in the distance something resembling the back of a huge turtle which they called The Mackinac. Hence, today, Mackinac Island.

It was here that the English built a fortress to withstand a raid by the Americans. This is known today as Fort Mackinac. England's occupation of the Island was short lived as the Americans recaptured it.

Copper Harbor in a more serene mood

A Sturdy Tree

This tree was planted in a tiny village of Lovke, nicely nestled in the valleys of Croatia, a Province of Yugoslavia. All the peoples of this particular region were peasants who worked especially hard to obtain their daily sustenance. Much of the valley was outlined with small houses and barns surrounded by picket fences. The barns usually sheltered a horse, cow, and if large enough, you would find some hogs. Of course, there were chickens scratching for food in every yard. I must tell you, too, that every household boasted about its garden whose produce was something to behold.

The summers in these parts were mild and beautiful and very conducive to an excellent and abundant fall harvest. The winters were quite similar to our Midwestern snows and temperatures.

In the late 1800s, there were some big economical changes in America particularly in the north. People, not only from this town, but also from other European countries learned about the great iron and copper boom. Thousands didn't hesitate to go to the New World to work, to build their homes and raise their families. The seaport in Hamburg, Germany was jammed with immigrants headed for the land of freedom.

There was a certain courtship between Martin Mihelich and Mary Bolf that began in this little settlement and it was a year or so later that these two neighboring Croats were married. In due time, a daughter was born named Vincenza. Word came from the land of plenty that all immigrants were employed the moment they set foot on this foreign soil. It didn't take the young married father too long to board the next ship to Ellis Island, an inspection point, and eventually to New York Harbor. After a short stop in this strange city, he stepped into a railroad coach and off to the wilds of northern Michigan, more precisely, to the town of Calumet, Michigan which was then known as the Copper Country. Today, some 90 years later, it still harbors this name. This is where the wearied traveler met up with his fellow Croats.

The new mother and daughter remained in the valley until the father found employment and a living compound. Perhaps six months to a year later, little Vincenza crossed the Atlantic with her mother who, at the time, wondered whether this voyage would bring them success and happiness.

It seems that all of Europe emptied itself into the new country and became a melting pot of Slavic people, the Scandinavian, the Italian, French, German, and those from Great Britain. The blazed trails now became a mecca of curious immigrants. As time went on, there were many misfortunes that plagued these foreigners such as mining accidents, illnesses, and the most devastating of which was the 1913 Christmas Eve holocaust in which 72 children had perished because of a false alarm fire.

There was employment for the heads of all households, most of whom worked in mines. Some chose lumbering and those who came from northern Europe became commercial fishermen.

The families grew in countless numbers such as the photo accompanying this story. This is a picture of Martin and Mary, the parents of Vincenza, on her wedding day, together with her brothers and sisters. There were two children missing from this photograph, one of whom was accidentally killed and the other died in infancy. You see, I too, belong to this sturdy tree, for these are my parents. I came into the world seven years after this happy event. I am fortunate, indeed, proud and grateful for being able to relate to my living kin and to all my readers about this flourishing family tree. As this tree stands, so do the roots continue to grow. This tree that was once planted in the ol' sod, has now borne much fruit. Throughout the many years, there have been many other trees that have enhanced this land of diverse tongues.

There were 3 yet to be

Another part of the tree

The tree is still growing

Doomed Staircase

The recent fire and loss of life in one of New York's shabby night clubs brings to mind of an incident that happened some 70 years ago in the village of Calumet, Michigan, my birthplace. Many accounts have already been written about this tragedy and recorded in the annals of Michigan history. Since I am a native of this territory and have had so many occasions to speak to other people about this most unfortunate happening, I personally am able to render a description of this gruesome event.

I must take you back again to this land of Lake Superior and give you a brief description of the people that lived there. What prompted me to give you this personal view is that four members of my immediate family were present and left me with this dismal message. What I am about to describe to you is an excerpt taken from a writing which I began a few years ago. Barring any health problems, its completion is forthcoming.

In this land of Copper Find, there were many Europeans who migrated to the United States in the late 1890s and early 1900s. Among these immigrants were the Slavic people of Yugoslavia, the native country of my parents, the Poles from Poland, The Czechs from Czechoslovakia. The Croats and Slovenes came from Northern Yugoslavia, the former of which was the mother tongue of my mother and father. There were other groups that formed this great line of migration, namely, the English from Cornwall, England, the French, the Italian, and the Scandinavian which comprise the Danes, the Swedes, the Norwegians, and their neighbors, the Finns. All these nationalities were the melting pot of the upper most part of the Upper Peninsula of Michigan known as the Copper Country.

During the influx of the immigration, there were many nationalities that went elsewhere in the Midwest such as Pennsylvania, Ohio, Illinois, Wisconsin, Minnesota and most of whom landed in Upper Michigan. The older members of my family told me that the territory in the early 1900s became vastly populated and this was primarily due to the mining of copper ore. The population exceeded 50,000 at that time. At this writing, I can't visualize so vast a figure to live in those parts. But a city it became and history was in the making.

Most of the Slavic people were tillers of the soil. I remember my father taking care of one milking cow, a few pigs and several chickens. The Scandinavians who came from the North Atlantic became expert commercial fisherman like their Viking ancestors. The French were experienced gardeners and the Italians were frugal gourmets. The English, known as the Cornish because of their Cornwald ancestry, were very knowledgeable about mining. With all the diverse experiences that these immigrants had, there was really one thing on their minds, namely, the mining of copper. No question about it, Calumet became Boom Town U.S.A.

Something very disappointing happened to all these good people. It was like an omen, "Go back to your country." So many adverse things occurred in their life, first, there were scores of miners that had lost their lives in the depths of the mines, then drownings, fires and the most catastrophic was the loss of 73 people at a Christmas Eve party in 1913. All victims, 62 children and 11 adults, suffocated at the bottom of a huge staircase. Why did this carnage happen? There were dissensions between the miners and the Mining Company which eventually caused a strike leading to the deaths of many citizens.

The Christmas gathering took place at the Italian Hall which was well known for its meeting place and entertainment. The hall on this fateful day was filled with happy faces indeed. It was a spacious place outlined by folding chairs occupied by scores of people, children, ladies with infants on their laps and the fathers of many families. Many ladies wore their wide brimmed hats while others wrapped their heads with babushkas. The men were seen sporting their trimmed mustaches. Most of the kids were running around losing themselves in the crowd. Some of them found a place where they were giving out candy which meant that there were continuous trips to this candy counter. For those who loved music for dancing and listening pleasure, there were always some in the crowd that knew how to play the accordion, the violin and the tamboritsa. Naturally, with this camaraderie came spirited beverage, cigar and cigarette smoke. There was much cheer in the air and all nationalities wished each other greetings and good health, especially God's blessings. In this noisy crowd, were my four sisters, Margaret, Mary, Anna and Victoria and a brother, Ladislav. It was getting a little late when two of them decided to leave for home. My brother and the latter two girls remained. Such was the scene just before the advent of the most devastating event in the history of the Copper Country.

The windows of this huge structure were partially opened due to the heavy cigarette smoke. There was a young man that was standing by one of the windows, evidently, getting some fresh air when he heard an outside passerby yell out, "Fire!" He, in turn, cried out the same and so did scores of others in the crowd. There was instant panic, mass hysteria, mass exit, utter confusion. There was one exit which was also the entrance. As far as it can be established, there was only one fire escape. The children were lost in this wild gathering but my two sisters were lucky to have found our brother who helped them down the fire escape. There was no fire, there was no smoke, other than the smell of grease coming from the kitchen. When the yelling, the hollering and the screaming ceased, those that survived were searching for their loved ones at the bottom of the staircase. The exit doors opened from within thus causing the suffocation of so many people. My uncle was on the top of this pile of flesh looking for his daughter, Eva. When he did locate her, he put her lifeless body on his shoulders and walked home. There was a friend of our family that had lost four members of his family. The perpetrator of this senseless act was never found, though tongues wagged and fingers pointed, yet no one was ever convicted. People in this mining town still talk about what took place that Christmas Eve. The markers at the local cemetery give lasting evidence of that day of infamy.

This unforgettable tragedy has been called the Italian Hall Massacre. Many years later, the building displayed graffiti depicting what horror transpired within on the Eve of Christmas 1913.

This hall of infamous bearing had an Italian background built by the early Italian settlers. It was used primarily for their business meetings, parties and dances. You can't imagine the ultimate in cuisine when different ethnic groups assembled for more festive occasions.

I recall going with my parents to this ballroom in the middle and late 20s only to watch most people stare into space as it was just a decade or so when many young lives were senselessly snuffed out at the foot of the stairs.

So many hard-working people in this populated village were terribly saddened by what took place and the families that were victimized seemed to have lived in seclusion which was also true at the home of my uncle where he and his family mourned the loss of their loved one.

As of 1988, the Italian Hall had undergone the misfortune of the wrecking ball and so the grim reminder stands no more much to the mind boggling of the natives of this striking community. However, their vivid imagination will never be erased.

The strike of 1913 had disturbed thousands of workers. It appeared that the mining of copper progressed at a snail's pace. Even the sight of lunch buckets tucked under the miners' arms was infrequent. Even the whistles of the local mines seemed to have been silenced. Then came another let down which certainly dampened the hearts of all the newcomers to this land of rich copper veins. The influenza of 1918 had taken a heavy toll of infant lives. And if all these recent omens didn't bewilder the builders of this rapidly growing Lake Superior country, then the events to follow in the late 20s and early 30s really stifled their economy.

A place of my sisters' rescue

The ill-fated Italian Hall

A night of horor

Funeral, of the Italian Hall Disaster

The Great Depression

I was a boy of ten or so when the economic world was changing and I wasn't that much aware of what was going on. I do know specifically though that many people were in want. There just wasn't any money to buy things. Jobs were very scarce and whatever was available the pay was low. We just can't fathom the idea of working for .35¢ an hour today.

Frankly, being an adolescent and active in all sorts of sports, the Depression was not primarily my concern. I knew that my parents, immigrants from Croatia, Yugoslavia, were troubled financially, and wondered what the next meal would be and where the next pair of overalls would come from once the pair you had on would wear out. Yes, it was a struggle and the older I became, I fully realized the impact this money pinch left on the local people. Sometimes one felt that only this part of America was deeply affected but others since then have told me that this part of Michigan was especially hit hard. So many people then said, "Make do with what you have."

A penny in this era was indeed a precious piece of copper like a gem to a ring bearer. Nickels and dimes were priceless commodities. Now that I am a senior retired teacher and still walking the Halls of Ivy, I often pick up pennies in the hall and reflect back some 60 years to learn what a few pennies would buy! I remember as a kid waiting for the Fourth of July to come around and I knew when the parade made that certain turn on Pine Street that there would be adults on this particular float throwing handfuls of pennies on the pavement and then the mad scramble for copper Indian Heads and Lincoln Heads. They were like tiny pieces of gold.

The few I did find were spent for something that all youngsters wanted, namely, candy.

To supply our household with food, my father, an avid hunter that he was, would kill deer and rabbits which in turn my mother would preserve the meat in glass quart jars. Since my father tended to a few hogs and chickens, our family would relish these meats also. The Scandinavians were great fishermen and it was they who taught me how to stream fish for trout, a sport of which I am still obsessed. But I do remember that trout was served at our table.

During the summer months, I picked berries such as wild strawberries, raspberries, thimble berries and blueberries. I was often asked by my mother to sell some of these berries to the well-to-do people of this village. This helped a little to buy other groceries. We always had jellies in the pantry. Summer time, too, was a time to "make wood" for the winter months. My father would take me to the woods and show me the art of chopping and sawing fallen timber. Undoubtedly, this is why I have a great love for the forest and all that it possesses and represents.

In the fall of the year, it was my chore to bag leaves which were used in our root house to keep the vegetables from frost. It was a time to prepare for the cold months ahead, chopping wood, putting up storm windows, you name it, it all had to be done, without pay, mind you.

Now for some playtime. We played hard and our bellies would be hungry for some of that homemade bread and jelly. We played a lot of baseball in big fields where the grass in the outfield would be almost knee deep. Quite a bit of time was spent just looking for the ball. Somehow, we managed to get a hold of a couple of gloves and bats. One of us would usually find a lost baseball where the village league played. That would be the only ball that we would have for a long time. I remember the ball being hit so many times that the cover would come off. Someone would volunteer to sew the ball and the next time the cover came off, we would use friction tape. This business of seek and find went on for months and even years.

In the evenings, the neighborhood gang played horseshoes under the location street light. My uncle who lived on the farm is the one that would provide the horseshoes. The pegs were much used drills from the local mines. Shortly after supper, we played the game of cricket which the people from Cornwall, England introduced.

In the winter, the Swedes, the Norwegians and the Finns would teach us how to skate and play hockey. They would always find some frozen dam, slough or pond and that's where the sticks would fly and the puck would be lost in the snowbank. Again, we would manage somehow to buy old skates and sticks. We would often wrap our shins with magazines fastened by bands of inner tubes which our fathers discarded. When hockey was not in play, we improvised small individual toboggans which were made from the staves of a barrel. Larger toboggans were made from a ten foot piece of corrugated tin. Those places then were hills which today would appear to be just mounds. These were the work and fun days of the Great Depression.

The other day, as I was leaving a restaurant, I noticed a homemade whistle at the side of the paying register. At that very instant, I couldn't help but go back during my childhood school days when every boy would carry on his person a pocket knife. On our way to school, there were some tag alder trees and shrubs from which we would make whistles. With these knives, we would also play the game of baseball which, at this moment, would require some instruction. Today, I just can't imagine one carrying a knife to school! Some lines back, I told you about the fun days. Well, I have another to tell you. The English folks brought another game of theirs from Europe. They showed us how to play marbles but it was not today's method. The game was played during the spring thaw when we used a marble shooter and commies. The latter of which were made from clay.

It was sometime after the crash that Franklin Delano Roosevelt put the country back on its feet with two projects that will be long remembered and cherished. The first of which was the Civilian Conversation Corps (CCC) begun in 1933. The second was the Works Progress Administration (WPA) begun in 1935. Their marks of success can easily be seen throughout the forests of Michigan.

I asked Mike Cain how the Depression affected the Niles area and he told me that its effect here was not as great as in the Upper Peninsula. "Niles was a very industrial town," he said and it was places like Kawneer, Simplicity, National Standard and the railroad that helped Niles during the economical struggle. He told me that jobs were still scarce. The farmers were spared the cost of food as they were self-sustained. They said that anyone not having enough money for theatre admission could give potatoes or eggs. After all, isn't money a means of exchange? Mike told me about the Michiana Theatres, The Ready, the Riviera, bank night at the Colfax, the Palace and the Strand. People talked a lot about baseball and softball and I remembered a buddy of mine from the Copper Country talking about Ike Bierwagen and Company and he said that he had never dreamed that there would be someone so awesome!

Some people told me that up in Muskegon, things were in bad shape. Many stood in line for food. As a matter of fact, the city bought food for its people. Some companies spotted their help. Top wages were a measly 35 - 50¢ an hour, sometimes less.

And so the Great Depression spent its awful moments in the Land of Copper. There was never any significant industrial revival in these parts other than the early Copper Boom. People learned what responsibility meant. They worked hard for very little compensation but were thoroughly satisfied. Their style of life was slow and very determined and didn't compete for personal glory. People cared for each other more than what we experience today. Borrowing food stuffs was a neighborly trait. When work picked up in the big cities, many left the confines or our tiny village to seek a comfortable living. The sons of many families would send money to their parents to ease the pain of poverty. Some would even come home to show off their brand new cars. The very young at home were always taught to improvise a tool for work or play. Truly it was a time long to be remembered for it taught us to live without, to respect our fellow man. It taught us responsibility and self discipline. There are moments today when I think, should there ever be another one, there would be no tomorrow.

The Keweenaw Miracle

Let me take you to the Land of Keweenaw. This is a piece of real estate that projects into the greatest fresh water lake in the world, Lake Superior. Some have called it the land of the Superior. Back in the late 1800s and early 1900s, this was Boomtown U.S.A. Many Europeans heard about a big copper find in this Keweenaw place. The first influx of immigrants came from Finland, Sweden and Denmark, then from Italy, France and Germany and the peoples from Poland, Slovenia and Croatia. Ellis Island became a momentary examination and resting area for thousands of tired and hungry peasants.

I am particularly proud that my parents were some of the passengers on the ocean liners that crossed the Atlantic. It was they that gave me a short history of these historic voyages. My father came to America as a young married man together with other ethnic groups searching for prosperity. His young bride came at a later date with their first-born daughter.

Calumet was the stopping place for the new arrivals. It wasn't too long before this tiny village became a growing colony and a melting pot of diverse languages. Being a native of this part of Michigan and also an immigrant offspring, I learned the cultures of other nations. During this time, work was plentiful, but hard and dangerous as all employees labored underground. Copper in this part of the world was rich and pure. These were good times now and people lived comfortably as there was enough food on the table and clothes warm enough to protect themselves from the long and cold winter blasts.

After the 1913 tragedy, the miners and their families lived in fear and want for several decades. They even survived the Great Depression and like so many others in America, they, too, lived a life of make-do without. Many people lived on welfare and on what little income was provided by some small industry. Most homes were simple frame structures as prescribed by mining company standards which are still evident today. It was rather obvious that these hard-working people sought only the meager means of livelihood. Most heads of the household were fishermen and hunters who provided much fish and meat for their families.

I return periodically to this land of retreat and I see people, places and things that I once saw some 60 years ago. I still recognize the many faces of senior citizens still maintaining their vigorous smiles but their bodies are bent and spent with age. Just standing in this mining town brings back a thousand memories.

Something big, really big, has happened in the Copper Country. The other day, my brother sent me some exciting news stating that our little village of Calumet has become a National Historic Park. The natives of this renowned town have hoped and prayed that some day security and economic growth would return. There came such a miracle growth. Not since the last load of rich copper ore coming from the veins of the belly of the earth was there such joy and jubilation when the President of the United States, George Bush, signed a Bill declaring their land an Historic piece of property.

There are still many natives of this small community that are able to tell us stories about the past. They take great delight in relating to the tourists about the famed stage personalities that have once graced the Calumet Theater. Those steeped in religious beliefs will take you to their many places of worship. Some of these buildings portray excellent workmanship. Your narrator will make it his business to tell you about the record snowfalls that buffets his country. And while he is describing this winter wonderland, he'd be happy to see you during one of their northern blasts. Next, he'll point in the direction of one of the copper mines that had entombed several miners during an underground fire. He will also tell you about several other mines in the vicinity. Washington High School and Morrison Elementary date back several decades and are still operable. The Calumet Armory still stands as living testimony of the headquarters of the early army and National Guard maneuvers. It is also the home of local hockey skirmishes.

I enjoy reminiscing with other Copper Country residents with whom I once walked to school when we'd watch miners going to work in the morning with lunch buckets tucked under their arms. Since we lived in this particular area, the miners were all headed toward one of the deepest mines on the range. We pictured them entering their skips which would take them down to various shaft levels. All their carbide lights were readied for their morning operation. Perhaps the most alarming moments of our boyhood companionship were the mine whistles blaring, telling all the families of this busy mining town that disaster had struck in one of the mines. There were many dark days when we'd see wreathes hanging on the front doors of the stricken families.

I am sure that there were many people and dignitaries responsible for this Keweenaw miracle. Without the slightest doubt, this was indeed a big face lift for this once thriving town. After much determination by our local and state officials, and by the final stroke of our Commander-in-chief's pen, this barren place was once again on the road to some prosperity.

At the Edge of Brevort Trail

The moon was smiling this one November evening during Michigan's annual deer hunt. There was a nip in the air and all was quiet, very quiet. It seemed that the dark night was flooded by the light of the full moon.

At dusk of the same day, I noticed the movement of a buck feeding at the edge of Brevort Trail in Mackinac County. I took careful aim with my 30-30 Winchester and fired. I waited a moment or two and walked to where the deer had stood and found that the animal was hit and crippled. There was a little snow on the ground and this is how I determined the bloodied trail of the deer. Since that early evening was also quiet, I could hear the young buck thrashing through the thicket. But it was time, I decided, to end my solo chase. I decided, then, too, to ask my brother-in-law, Ted, to help me continue the search sometime after supper. His daughter, Yvette, an outdoor adolescent craze, also volunteered for the rendezvous in the wilds

It must have been about nine or ten o'clock when we began our tracking operation. We started our maneuver where I first spotted the yearling buck. I should note that Ted's daughter enjoyed the wilderness. As we proceeded, we spoke very little, and if so, it was in a hush so as not to alert the deer's flight. There were times that we almost tiptoed along even though we knew that the whitetail was well on his way.

I heard Ted say, "We're getting close." I was right beside him when I answered, "Yeah, you can almost smell his tracks." There were several other deer tracks around but the set we looked for showed signs of a leg dragging. Yvette wondered when all this would come to an end. Her voice quivered a bit when she said, "It's cold out here."

The moon was as bright as ever and as we sneaked through the timber, we noticed its brightness flicker in our faces. This business of tracking deer was truly exhilarating and at this writing, we are just days away for another firearm season which brings back a thousand memories of sloshing in November's moonlit night.

There was a new blanket of snow that had covered our terrain over night. You might have guessed that bright and early the next day I made a beeline to the place of last night's commotion. There was much water in a nearby swale and I had assumed that this was where the deer had bedded down for the night to heal its wounds. I was greeted abruptly by the splash of our ghost in the night. I was a bit saddened though that we never did locate this fleeting phantom.

Some three decades have passed since I last kicked the sod of the trail that leads to our moonlight rendezvous. I am sure that there are many untold stories about man and the elusive whitetail. Stories that only the Brevort bunch could tell.

Since we are so close to the edge of this unforgotten trail, I must tell you of another incident not too distant from the sighting of the spikehorn. I thought of something amusing one late afternoon while sitting on a small ridge. I was curious to know just how much company I had near me at this time of day. It was at this moment that I stepped out into a clearing, pointed my gun skyward and let go a volley of shots. In a matter of seconds, I came face to face with an army of excited nimrods.

A Hunting Obsession

Since I personally have become closely associated with a certain group of hunters back in the middle 50s, I find it to be a happy moment for me to write about all the characters who filled that vast stage in Mackinac County. More specifically, the Brevort Trail, the Pipeline, the Black Top, and the Brevort River Bridge that once was. I am certain that those who read this particular column and who were members of the Brevort Camp will remember all those places!

Not like the camps of wood blocks and running water, these hunters were city folks and even after they arrived in this old Indian country, they lived like city slickers back home. Make no mistake about it though, they loved the wilds and enjoyed hunting and were always sure about their target. They did not live in tents or log cabins but these guys all hung their caps and coats in motels and ate their meals at a small restaurant just adjacent to the motor lodge. Some years, there were 30 sharp shooters that visited Brevort Camp. In the course of four years or so, we all became close friends. Our rendezvous was located 20 miles west on U.S. Highway 2.

As you well know, at every camp there is a leader of some sort who takes it upon himself to point out all the good hunting places and those that 'aint't' so good. I believe that it was that same leader that was responsible for platooning other men to come up to this region to hunt deer. While I'm on the subject of telling people where to hunt deer, I must tell you about another hunter that used to have a chalk board at camp to tell his hunters where to go. How would you like to take that route?

194

When all the company arrived, you were there to touch glasses, play cards and have some hard laughs. Now you know that every camp gets into some heated discussions such as trying to find out the best place to go in the morning. Someone would suggest to go north of Worth's Road and his reply would be, "Nah, you don't know what you're talking about and, besides, I looked around there yesterday and didn't see anything." This would go on for hours while playing cards. Come morning, all the previous evening's decisions were scrubbed which meant you made your own choice and as you well know, that was and still is big country!

There were some relatives in the gang. Two of which lived in that area the entire year and the other lived in Niles. All three were great outdoor sportsmen. The oldest of whom was an excellent marksman. The youngest of the trio was the proud owner of a truck named Big Sid about which we will speak in detail later. The third knew the tricks of hunting.

It seems that at every camp there was a stumbling block of some sort. I remember one that we had when I hunted with my father in Keweenaw County. He owned a '34 Ford which on many occasions, was loaded with hunters and buck carcasses trying to climb a very steep hill plowing through a foot of new snow. We'd be some distance from the hill to get a good 'running' start and then get to about midway up the hill and that would be it! After three tries, the car's engine would be sapped and we, too, would be exhausted from laughing so much. The hunters at Brevort had their problems, too. Sometime in the early 50s, there was an oil pipeline that was installed in Mackinac County stemming from one of the northern Canadian Provinces. It so happened that this line crossed the original Brevort Trail which made travel really rough because of the soft sand. This is when Big Sid entered the picture. Being that the vehicle was heavy to begin with, plus the weight of 10 guys and their rifles, the short trip across the pipeline was barely made, and I do mean barely.

Some distance behind, there was a much lighter pickup truck and that, too, was loaded with a bunch of laughing people. The driver would put the truck in first then second and third gear some two to three hundred feet from the oil line and took off as though he was being chased by a posse. No, sir, it was just not to be, as it, too, sank in the sand. There were enough bodies around helping to jack the truck digging by hand and shovel, throwing branches, logs and what have you underneath the wheels. Finally, the end of the struggle came after many tries. This went on every day as long as the troops stayed. At one point, it looked like a convoy of red-coats.

Big Sid was the trail blazer as it plowed through rust, brush and trees and I'm sure that other hunters could have heard them laughing some ridges beyond. What was Sid's destination? The black top, of course, which was just a small piece of hardened tar laid during the construction of the pipeline. Today, it is still there and if one were to inspect it closely, he would perhaps find the initial of the one who named it.

Not too far beyond this marker, still on Brevort Trail, was an old dilapidated bridge crossing Brevort River the mouth of which was Lake Michigan. This is where one of you, at age 19 then, had shot your first buck. I could tell that you dragged it some distance as your face was the same color as your coat.

Father and son at deer hunting camp
in the early '50's

Big Frank

They called him Big Frank not so much because of his stature, even though he was tall and lean, but he just did things in a very big way. To begin with, he was of German descent and all matters had to be executed according to his plan. He had that Prussian way about him and all his plans were engineered promptly and flawlessly. Anyone that worked under his jurisdiction eventually became an accomplished disciple.

Most of Frank's life was laboriously spent in Moran, Michigan, a small whistle stop in early Mackinac County. Everyone knew Big Frank to be a hard working man. Since it was a tiny community just north of the Straits of Mackinac, this man knew all the townspeople and all their occupations. In spite of all the derogatory impressions that people may have had about him, he was still faithful about keeping the Lord's Day. I had the pleasure of meeting him in the late 40s and not only did I respect this towering character, but I also cherished his friendship.

At one point in his early life, he became the local car dealer. He would always display a new model in his tiny congested showroom (you might say showing off the latest model in the Oldsmobile division). It would usually be the car that someone had recently ordered. His place of business was also a garage or an extensive workshop. This proud man worked hard and he took such great pride in his little repair factory. Believe me, he was some kind of mechanic! I picture this dynamic person teaching today's auto mechanics class. Whatever he fixed, it stayed that way. Harold, his son-in-law, back in the 40s was just a novice in this welding room, but as the many years passed, he, too, was a skilled worker with cars, tools and machinery.

I remember my first visit in Big Frank's Garage. It was like walking into the archives of documented tools. There were several rows of shelving containing kits for tune-ups, inner tubes and patching and new tires still wrapped up in brown paper and tools of all makes and calibres. This was definitely a repair shop as you could see so many things strewn about that needed some repair. It was not the cleanest of places, but I can assure you that what came out of that place was guaranteed. Being that this building had so many collectible items, and if it still existed today, it would be ravaged like the piranhas of the Amazon River.

I must tell you that I think of Frank's place quite often as this is where I learned to laugh. I learned so many things by watching, listening and talking. In this workshop, there was a potbelly stove which, during the cold winter months, was going full blast along with this man's stories. Most of us would stand by the stove warming our hands and turning around to warm our backs. Frank's ice fishing stories were classics and my only regret at the moment is that no one ever recorded his words of outdoor wisdom. At the moment of this writing, I am desperately trying to remember what had transpired in this town's garage back in the good ol' days! I do know, though, that when the stories were being told, the coffee pot was never empty. There's no question that when the ol' timer told his story, his gestures were so unique and this is why life around that stove was so hilarious. This was a hunting and fishing town and whoever had the floor would talk about the big musky that he landed at Brevort Lake, or about the limit of trout he caught at Carp River, even the snowshoe rabbits his beagles would corral along the town's railroad tracks, or even about dragging that huge buck he shot that year. And when these outdoor stories would be exhausted, they'd talk about new and used cars. When Frank and Company worked on a used car, you wouldn't dare to question their ability of workmanship. Just as one entered this "house of many memories", there was an old gasoline pump that was still very much in use. All the gas was pumped by hand which was clearly visible on the top. As you passed the premises, you were reminded that there was a blacksmith at work. I asked myself, "What couldn't this man do?" I can still hear the ring of the anvil on which he would mold shoes for the farmers' horses in rural Mackinac County or he'd be making a strip for a logger's trailer hitch. The ol' timer knew that I enjoyed ice fishing and from that same anvil, came a spear that bewildered all the Northern Pike of Brevort Lake and Époufette Bay!

The story of this most invigorating man would not be complete without my telling you about his engineering feat during the ice harvest on Brevort Lake. Naturally, he was in command and when his crew did as he directed, it was almost a work of art to see this ice being cut by a motor-driven 36" saw. I just stood there in wonderment as they pulled those square blocks of ice from the water using cant and ice hooks and from there, transported to sawdust-filled ice sheds. The younger set probably tagged along to see how thick the ice was and wondered why the waters looked so cold and deep. It was a happy life in this small railroad town in the 40s and I'm sure that the natives still talk about the good ol' days!

Ice fishing at Brevort Lake

Model A 1930 -- what a car!

Lake Superior

As I write you these lines, another winter has passed in Southwest Michigan. Since there are still many traces of snow in parts further north, I would like to tell you about the snows that harbor the shores of Lake Superior. This is the territory that the first "copper-boomers" named as the Copper Country.

Most readers would not believe how relentless the winters are in this part of the Great Lakes region. If it does not snow, then its natives are disturbed, thinking perhaps that the gods had intervened.

I remember so vividly when I was a little boy how my mother used to dress me to get ready for school. All the clothing she wrapped me with was made out of wool. Once the long johns were in order, then the wool shirt, trousers, overcoat, which back then was called a mackinaw, the swampers (footwear), the mitts, the cap which covered my ears and part of my face and the last piece of winter equipment was the scarf which she wrapped around my neck and face. This was almost a daily ritual as winter meant real business. Why all this because of some snow? There was a blizzard out there and besides school was open all day. When I left the house, the only thing that had human resemblance were my eyes peaking through all that clothing. I had a small lunch box dangling in my hands. I was thinking more of what was inside than facing the north wind. It wasn't too long before I caught up with the neighborhood kids. The trek to school took about a half hour. All of us lived in the outskirts of our little village and as we walked to school, we looked like mountain climbers forming a line. As I trudged along, I thought of the pennies that my mother gave me to buy candy during recess. The candy store was just a skip from the school grounds. A penny's worth was almost enough to pass around in the classroom to be eaten after hours!

After school, the teacher would help us get dressed and our group would all get together for the walk back home. With all the school work behind us and the long journey to our homes, we were so exhausted when we opened the kitchen door. The first thing that I remember doing was making a beeline to the pantry where I knew that there was homemade bread and jellies. Those were the good ol' days!

The north wind was still howling when I came in and the house seemed to have swayed a bit. All the spaces where the cold would seep through were plugged with some cloth and there would always be something on the floor by the door to keep the cold out. It was always my chore to see to it that both woodbins would be filled before nightfall. We had a heatrola stove in the living room that would heat both that area plus the upstairs via registers. The stove in the kitchen was the champion of them all, the good ol' cook stove which made bread, pies and pastries. The latter of which was a dish originated by the people of Cornwald, England. That kitchen stove, incidentally, was not only an excellent cooker but also a great space heater. As I sit here pounding away at these thoughts, I can still smell the coffee that my mother and father brewed every morning before sunup.

Before I make you too uncomfortable with winter talk, I must tell you one more thing about those cold, cold nights in the land of the Copper Country. When all of us would get up in the morning, every single window of our house was heavily frosted, so much so, that we did not know what it was like outdoors. After melting a small section with our warm breaths, about the size of a half dollar, we would learn about the works of mother nature. Our house was barricaded by a mountainous snowdrift. The path leading to the main road would always be covered with new snow, so much so, that at nightfall, you did not know if you were on the path or not. I remember my father engineering a way to recognize the path at all times. He would tell us to use snowshoes to thoroughly pack the snow. The trail, so to speak, was then outlined by chopped saplings which made the course easier to find.

Living in the vicinity of this vast body of water, I am able to tell you about its serenity, its beauty and its violent moods. I has been known to swallow anything that is in its path of destruction.

I recall, during the falls days, sitting in the back yard of our home and looking in the direction of the Big Lake watching the formation of dark storm clouds. With this foreboding atmosphere, came the sound of rough seas. I knew at this very moment that there were loaded iron ore freighters plowing and fighting their way from Duluth headed for the steel factories at Detroit or the steel mills of Gary, Indiana. At the same time, there were empty ore boats whose compasses were pointed to the western shores of this great natural spring.

Lake Superior is noted for its large deposits of Agate stone which was formed by the early glaciers. This stone is sought by many rock hounds and the experts in this field tell us that the best time to search for this "gem" is when Old Superior coughs up its pebbles after a violent storm. As a youngster, I often combed the shores at Five Mile and Seven Mile Points and also Copper Falls in Keweenaw County searching, digging and pushing aside larger stones to locate this "glacier diamond."

It is impossible for me to tell you just how much time I spent looking and gazing at this magnificent creation and how many times my relatives and I have camped by it listening to its summer laps. In the fall, these same laps would turn into midnight madness. Even that was beautiful. I have even smelled its fury.

Now for a bit of adventure. Back in '48 or so, near the extreme western shores of Lake Superior, near the town of Ironwood, I was invited to do some deep-sea fishing for lake trout. I really wasn't that enthused about sailing this big lake on an 18' inboard motor boat but my friend, Vic, assured me that we'd have a nice time catching trout. Of course, his best friend, a black Labrador Retriever, also came along. It was the one that really enjoyed the water the most! It was a calm day when we started and we decided to go out about five miles. We trolled for about a half hour or so when I noticed some dark clouds on the horizon. This is when I yelled, "Vic, head for shore!" It wasn't too long after that, that we were engulfed by the huge swells of this unpredictable lake. Luckily, we were being pushed to shore by this sudden squall. We still had power on the small craft even though the rudder was out of the water most of the time. You might have known that the Lab was in his glory, resting his paws on the edge of the boat, panting and looking at the sea gulls while we were being aimlessly tossed about. Believe me, there were moments when I thought we were going to be swallowed into the belly of mighty Superior. Yes, this was surely the time for meditation!

You must believe me when I tell you that this Great Lake shows no mercy and has no concern for the inventions of modern man. Its big and strong gale forces come early and with them, come ice, snow and freezing temperatures. In many instance in the past, this has been S.O.S. time! This mighty one of them all has taken its toll on ships that have been smashed by striking reefs or shoals or ships that have been split in two with total loss of life and cargo. It has been said that the areas of Eagle Harbor and Copper Harbor are often called the Mariners' Graveyard. In the heat of its fury, one is almost deafened by its thunder and lashing.

At this point of my account of this Great Lake, I would like to tell you about some ships that fell prey to these great waters. Shipwrecks were many, in the hundreds they say, stretching from the Kewennaw Peninsula to Marquette, Grand Marais and Whitefish Bay. Ships have also been lost in the vicinity of Isle Royale, an island belonging to Michigan some 55 miles from the mainland and 15 miles from the Canadian shores.

Traveling in Keweenaw County on M-26 along the Big One you will see Grand Marais Harbor. It was at this spot that I saw "the leftovers" of a Canadian barge that had been hauling pulpwood destined for a paper mill. The tug that was pulling the load had already been removed. Unfortunately, the wife of the skipper perished when the tug was thrown against the reef. When the storm subsided, all that was left were pulp logs strewn and floating in the Harbor. In addition, the barge was leaning precariously on one of the Harbor's large rocky walls.

Undoubtedly, the most catastrophic of Lake Superior shipwrecks was the sinking of the Edmund Fitzgerald on November 10, 1975 off Whitefish Bay northeast of the Soo Locks. To this day, its disappearance still remains a mystery though there are many speculations about the cause of this great loss. Today, it quietly rests on the floor of this Great Lake entombing 29 hands aboard. In navigation circles, it has been said that Lake Superior keeps her dead. I am certain that every seaman who has ever sailed this piece of water and every captain that has his hands on the helm of a ship know that they cannot and must not underestimate its incredible strength.

It is also true that every novice sailing this 600 mile long lake is aware of what a gigantic swell has done and can do to man's unsinkable ships!

And now for my final thoughts about this Mecca of beauty, thunder, sport and retreat. In the late 1880s, various Indian tribes fished the St. Mary's Rapids which was the body of water running from Superior to Lake Huron. Before the

Soo Locks came to be, the height of the rapids extending over a mile was 22 feet which every ship going through the Locks today must either be elevated or lowered, depending upon its direction.

We are now in the land of the Chippewas, Algonquians, Ojibwas and Potawatomis. I was rather fortunate indeed to witness a recent powwow in which these tribes participated. I am sure that I was watching the Indians whose ancestors once fished for Menominee whitefish in the St. Mary's Rapids. At this Indian gathering, there was much drumming, singing and dancing by the red men from all parts of the Midwest particularly from the neighboring Reservations at Sugar Island and Bay Mills. It was fascinating to see their array of colored feathers and variety of hides of wild animals. I pictured their dances of yesteryear symbolizing peace, good harvest, death, birth and marriage.

In our panoramic visit to beautiful Lake Superior, we began in the land of iron ore, through our copper mines, passing the treacherous reefs of Keweenaw, entered the dangerous waters of Grand Marais in Luce County, viewed the Pictured Rocks at Munising, and sailed cautiously from Marquette through the depths of Whitefish bay and proudly concluded that all this was Superior Land.

Calumet's local Milwaukee road depot

On the way to Keweenaw in the winter

The Pioneers of the Copper Country

Sam and Martin Mihelich left their fatherland at an early age. Good news came to their tiny village nestled in the hills and valleys of Croatia. It was news from America. Many from this country and the surrounding principalities left their meager farmlands to seek a prosperous future.

They were hard working people, each family owning just a small parcel of land on which they grew vegetables to sustain life, a cow to give them milk and cheese, chickens to provide them with meat and eggs and just a few hogs to enrich their food supply.

Sam and Martin were brothers who married two sisters shortly before their departure to the New World. It was rather unique that both sisters gave birth to a daughter prior to their voyage to America.

Back in the late 1800s, there were many passenger liners and cattle ships that sailed the Atlantic toward New York Harbor. On these steamships, were diverse cultures comprised of the Swedes, Finns, Danes, Germans, French, Italians, Poles, Slovenes, Croats and Norwegians.

It wasn't too long after their landing in this strange country that these two young exuberant men found some temporary employment. Both were hired as saloon caretakers, evidently helping their proprietors moving beer, wine and whiskey barrels. They also had the despicable job of cleaning spittoons, especially after spitting contests when patrons would often miss their targets. Back in those days, chewing and spitting tobacco juice was quite an art. There was a certain ring in the spittoon when one did hit his mark!

Both of these foreigners became rather skilled in their work so much so that they invested in the tavern business. Martin chose to remain in the village of Calumet but his older brother, Sam, traveled some 15 miles further north to a small location known as Phoenix. There he also managed a General Store. It really didn't matter where one would establish his business as thousands of immigrants poured into this land of rich copper and the economy was in full swing. There were scores of mines in operation at full tilt. And, today, almost a century ago remnants still stand as grim reminders of the good and bad times.

Several years later, this little curve on the gravel road became the permanent home for Sam and his growing family.

There is so much to tell you about these two pioneers so I will begin with the younger of the two. Young Martin became a noted hunter in those parts. You would often see this mustached European sporting his twelve gauge shotgun accompanied by his favorite rabbit hound. His cap was of the Tyrolean style probably resembling that of his fellow Croats back home in the old country. You might say that back in 1905, he blazed many hunting trails for himself and his many friends.

Besides his work in the local saloon, he also worked in the mines. However, that was short lived since one of his older brothers who preceded him to this country perished while working underground. This changed his attitude and his work. There were many many others who met the same fate.

Since there was an influx of immigrants moving in this part of Michigan, Martin became steadily employed as a drayline operator which in today's way of life, would be one experienced in hauling freight. It was indeed a thriving business. He owned a sturdy wagon and a team of draft horses to transport the belongings of these homesick and weary travelers. On one such occasion his son accompanied him, riding on the very top of the load of bags, suitcases, tables, chairs and makeshift beds when something or someone startled the horses. The sudden lunge moved the load and the 11 year old passenger fell to the ground. It was a little while later that his father checked to see how things were riding when much to his dismay, he noticed his son on the ground wincing in great pain. It was discovered that the rear wheel of the wagon had run over the boy's abdomen. The father carried his boy home where he died three days later. This incident became very troublesome to the parents and the rest of the family. So much so that the father was often found to be in a meditative state.

Since he enjoyed hunting, I was told that he provided well for the family table showing baked bird, rabbit and venison. Much of the wild game, too, was preserved in glass jars. He also enjoyed working in the garden and maintaining a few livestock. Rhode Island Reds were his favorite.

There are still some folks around this village that talk about him and his love of the wilds and how he enjoyed the camaraderie of his fellow Slavs. I was told, too, that he was quite eloquent about world affairs.

All that he knew about the forest, the wilds, the art of camping under lean-to's and about roughing it, he taught his five sons. Each time he returned from a day's hunt, he not only smelled of the forest but he was also the forest sentry.

You see, this man, this foreigner from the tiny village of Lokve, Croatia, this mustached sentry was my father.

A classic portrait of this man of the forest currently graces the home of my sister. Whether this treasure will ever honor my home remains to be seen. On it, there is an inscription that reads in the Croatian language, "Bili na lovu", meaning "We were hunting." The historical photo was taken by my father's lifelong hunting companion John Malnar on October 10, 1905.

His older brother, Sam, loved farming. There is so much to be said about this man as he was so gentle, not only with his fellow man but also with the animals whether they be domestic or wild. Sam was tall and lanky and as far back as I can remember, he always sported a goatee which evidently became his mark of distinction. I recall so vividly when our families would get together during the summer months to work in the hay fields. Homemade cooking became a customary feast for all of us. There was a small stream that meandered just below his house and this is where I first learned how to swim. And since I enjoyed the confines of a trout stream, I would always manage to wet my line in a creek that flowed just a short distance from the ol' homestead. During our visits there, Sam's team of draft horses, Storm and King, by name, would inevitably impress me. You could tell that he was proud of them.

His farm covered quite a bit of acreage most of which was put into hay. Like his brother, Martin, he had a large garden. He also raised sheep which when sheared, the wool was sold to help his family financially. There are places in our state that have sheep today and I must admit that my thoughts bring me back to Sam's sheep grazing those small rolling hills. I recall one year when my mother was given some wool and it didn't take her too long to make a quilted comforter.

The cold Canadian north wind blasts were on the prowl on the night of November 30, 1926. Some 25 miles north of the copper spur of Phoenix, lies Lake Superior, the world's greatest fresh water lake. It was hit hard that night, it became relentless. There were shipping companies that were a bit reluctant about putting their ships out to sea especially at this time of year. However, there were others that would try to push as much cargo across the lake before the deep freeze.

On this memorable day, the freighter, City of Bangor, carrying a load of new 1926 Chryslers, was fighting her way through ice, sleet and snow. As the ship was nearing Keweenaw Point, she slammed into one of the reefs. The

Coast Guard found her encased in ice the next morning while its crew found shelter and warmth in the dense forest off shore. When news of this disaster reached the small farming regions, there were nearby farmers who came to the rescue to remove the cargo from the ship. Among these courageous men who braved the stiff breezes with their teams of horses plowing through snowdrifts was Sam. You might have guessed that Storm and King were there, too.

In my brief research of Lake Superior shipwrecks, I found an interesting segment about the City of Bangor. I was so pleased to recognize a figure sitting on a wood block, evidently taking a break from hauling those cars. I can tell you one thing though, that goatee of his was as white as the snow that was around him.

The avid hunter

Brothers 5

The inseparable

Forts Michilimackinac and St. Joseph

During the Revolutionary era, it seems that wars among the Indian tribes, wars between the French and English and the English and Americans were all inevitable.

Fort Michilimackinac back in 1776 was a British garrison and also an excellent trading post. Since it was located on the shores of Lake Michigan, there was much canoe traffic made by the English, French and Indians. One can imagine the sentries being on the lookout for the enemy coming from the direction of the "Big Turtle's Back" or from any other part of this mighty lake. Even in winter, the soldiers could not completely rest. If the wind was right, war drums could be heard from miles around.

After the English defeated France in the French and Indian War, there were thousands of English, Indians and French-Canadians that had traded at the Fort. You might have guessed that since whiskey flowed like water, that there was much cheating and fraud during the fur trades.

At no time during my writings will I give you a thorough study of the strifes and conflicts that existed between the various nations that were represented at the Forts but rather give you a bird's-eye view that such posts did display their flags and life in and around their compounds.

It is most interesting to note the style of life that was evident during that era. Many people carried furs. Indians, particularly in winter, traveled on snowshoes as they were the makers of this fine art. Some carried huge chunks of birch bark which were the makings of this snow wear. It is hard to imagine the treacherous travels on the high seas of Lakes Michigan and Huron. The swift rapids of uncharted rivers, life in the cold blizzardy winter nights, the guns and ammunition that spelled instant death, sickness and the many diseases that brought lingering death. All this because of man's greed.

Dissention between the Indian tribes and the British had been brewing for quite some time. Chief Pontiac was very much aware of this and became rather angry. For this reason, he summoned a parley and believe me, nobody was smoking a peace pipe! The French and the Indians on the other hand, were always on friendly terms. So much so that they intermarried.

In June 1763, there was a plan to trick the English at Fort Michilimackinac. The Indians invited the soldiers to watch a game of LaCrosse. Being that this was the King's birthday, the regiment was in 'good spirits.' This was a game that was first adopted by the North American Indian. It was indeed a rough game played only by the warriors. Each player had a stick with a net on its end to catch the ball. During this particular skirmish, the soldiers were deeply engrossed in the sport and all this while, the Indian women and their children along with those carrying the unborn sneaked into garrison concealing in their garments tomahawks and knives. The moment for the massacre came when the ball was deliberately tossed into the compound. The bloody ordeal was short and quick and only the Captain and a few soldiers were spared.

During the raid, the Indians took whatever they pleased. At the end, Fort Michilimackinac was destroyed by fire. This was Pontiac's most triumphant moment. Since then, the drums have been silent. The Fort today, had been restored to its original plan and the landscape is still a grim reminder of what took place on the morning of a faked LaCrosse game.

There are still many full-blooded Indians living in and around Mackinac and Emmet Counties. And because of the close ties of the French and Indian people, one will find even today many French-Indian settlers. It was during my short sojourn in this territory that I befriended the descendents of the early fur traders with whom I fished, hunted and broke bread.

Fort St. Joseph was quite a distance from the top of the Lower Peninsula of Michigan. There was a small stronghold built around the close of the seventeenth century along the banks of the St. Joseph River where our city of Niles now thrives. The Potowatamis weren't too friendly at first as they attacked the settlement about the same time when Pontiac annihilated the English at Fort Michilimackinac. Fort St. Joseph became a very strategic point in this area besides being a flourishing trading post. Getting to the Fort by land, one had to slosh through bayous, meadows and swamps. This is where the Silverbrook and St. Joseph River met.

It was during this time, too, that the French Jesuit Missionaries had christianized hundred of Indians as was the case in the upper part of the state.

Fort St. Joseph was indeed a busy station and had you been a witness to its transactions, you would have seen hundreds of French, English and bands of red men talking, selling and buying commodities that were either obtained in the New World or carried over from the Old.

I am certain that because of Fort St. Joseph, Niles became the City of Four Flags. First, the French flag, a white piece of cloth was raised to declare its takeover. Then the English, under the command of Ensign Schlosser, placed their colors and when Spain heard about some trouble around the fort, it raised its flag and at the termination of the Revolutionary War, our Stars and Stripes became the final victor.

My bibliographical sketches were taken from the Old Fort St. Joseph by Ralph Ballard; At The Crossroads by Amor and Widder; and My State And Its Story by Ferris E. Lewis.

Nostalgic Moments

It seems that in all my writings, I get carried away about people and things especially about the past. There are so many memories of yesteryear, people that are still alive to tell us what happened a long time ago. True, books do tell us what took place years ago, but isn't it so much more interesting when your storyteller is standing or sitting right beside you? Today, I would like to review some photos that I recently observed in one of our doctor's offices.

I marvel at the many abandoned barns, some that still stand as a living memory of an era when milking cows roamed and grazed our pastures, some stored with tons of hay and so many today have already collapsed because of age and strain.

Do you remember the vegetable gardens which were the pride and joy of every family on the block? Today's garden enthusiasts have copied what they once saw as they were growing up and now they are inviting their friends to come see their organic miracle!

Remember when you were just a kid on your first tire swing and then a few years later, your father built you a swing that helped you reach the sky!

Each time that I see a water pump, I think of the one that my family had in the kitchen and another one outdoors near the entrance to the house. It was by this outdoor one that I spent many hot summer days pumping and drinking spring water from a metal cup or ladle.

The flower garden flanking your house was the work not only of your caring mother but also your father whose jobs were to annually beautify your landscape.

How could you forget the ice cream parlors in your vicinity? A bunch of you kids would run to your favorite spot and if you lived too far, there would always be someone around to give you a lift either by horse and buggy or by the people who had just bought a new Model T Ford.

Feeding the chickens may have been your chore, but fetching the eggs was more fun. Do you remember the different kinds of chickens you had, the Plymouth Rocks, the Rhode Island Reds, the Leghorns, and the New Hampshires all picking up goodies in the front and back yard. In the spring of the year, you fondled the little chicks that your father had behind the cookstove.

Do you remember the creek that meandered by your farmland property and the trout you use to catch for breakfast?

Next came harvest time the occasion to preserve tomatoes, beets, pickles, cherries, pears, peaches and many jellies.

Making hay while the sun shines were two months of the summer that you will long remember.

How about that one winter morning when you got up, you noticed that your '45 Ford was practically buried by an evening blizzard?

You can't erase those memories of approaching your house from a slight incline in the road. The view was breath-taking this one fall day when an early snow covered your spread.

Can you recall going to the local butcher shop for your mother and picking out a slab of bacon that smelled and tasted like bacon?

Back in the 40s, everyone listened to the news on the radio as well as the Hit Parade and other favorite programs. While you listened, you also stared at the box as though it was a TV!

For my final bit of nostalgia, I would like to take you to a small town in Upper Michigan and visit with me a General Store. It was indeed a very busy corner in this tiny farming community. I have never forgotten this place and it is deeply implanted in my mind. I'm sure that most of you are familiar with such a store. Besides selling things, it was also a U.S. Post Office. Since I knew the manager of this establishment, I often stopped in to chat and I used to watch him waiting on people especially when he had to use that long handled hook to grab merchandise from the top shelf.

But the most memorable moments of my being there was the arrival of two brothers who came in to do their weekend shopping. They reminded me of two grubby people who lost sight of the importance of water! I was so inquisitive about their identity that I just had to ask the proprietor who they were and where they lived. "Oh, those two guys, they live up the road a bit in a house that has farm animals living in it and the padlocked shack has no floor and they live in there, too!" Naturally, I drove by their house and got a real good glimpse of some of the strange aspects of the life lived in the late 40s.

The unforgetable cook stove

221

Every home had one

Heatrola, a winter's delight

The Smell of Balsam

The month of December leaves me with fond nostalgic moments. I was just a boy in my early teens when I tramped through the deep snows of the Upper Peninsula in search of a balsam that would eventually be destined to stand next to our upright piano. I do not ever remember it ever being elsewhere. I do recall, however, that my mother was the sole engineer as to its exact location.

Getting ready for my jaunt was most exciting. I left the house geared with a small hatchet and rope which were tucked under my mackinaw. My pockets, of course, bulged with homemade bread and strawberry sandwiches and some lunch meat. I snowshoed to the places that I had frequented during the fall season when the fir trees showed their finest stature. It didn't take me too long before I found my prize. It was a beauty! While I walked around it admiring its well formed limbs, I found a windfall that I used for my snack stool. While I enjoyed my goodies, I was enthralled by my surroundings which included the birch, hemlock, oak and maple trees along with the many tracks of weasels, snowshoe rabbits and deer. All this left me with a question as to how an Infinite Being could make these things be and to cause such wonderment!

The air was cold and crisp and in the distance you could hear the snap of a tree which was jolted by the bitter cold. It was time now for the proud task of chopping down this beautiful balsam. The first stroke of the hatchet brought a chip sapped with an aroma that was most pleasing. It was just a matter of minutes and my tree was felled. During this

223

lumberjack maneuver, I had my .22 rifle leaning against an adjacent tree and ready for a fleeting snowshoe hare.

When I reached a certain age, it was my responsibility to see to it that there would be a Christmas tree ready for another season. This no longer became a chore but indeed a pleasure. I do have fond recollections on other occasions when I would take along my improvised toboggan made out of corrugated tin. Being heavily waxed, it made my pull so much easier. Besides loading my tree, I also gathered up some dead cedars which were used for kindling wood for our kitchen and living room wood stoves. In the not too distant past, this course of action would have amazed the modern world but with our present energy pinch, it has copied the primitive way of life.

On my way home from these woodland journeys, I managed to ride down some small hills with the tree and wood well anchored. Had I known the Christmas ballad, "I'll Be Home For Christmas," I no doubt would have hummed its tune all the way to the living room. Snowshoeing and pulling my load, I thought of all the joy that accompanies the Yuletide. The songs, games, skiing, skating, hockey, rabbit hunting, snowball fights and digging snow tunnels that looked like mine shafts. Even household chores became a pleasure as I knew that in a matter of an hour or so, I would be rolling down a huge snowbank.

The smell of our freshly cut balsam filled our little home with a special fragrance that lasted for weeks. Once the tree was on its stand, I would often pinch a twig or a cluster of needles to get that extra aromatic pleasure. Since then, the fir family holds a special place in my memories.

Promptly at 6 p.m. on Christmas Eve, my mother would begin her decorating ritual. This was her custom as a child in Europe and I am sure that had she been living today, things would be the same. Christmas for her was truly Christian in every sense of the word. Her decorations, ornaments, trimmings and tinsels were old and beautiful yet ornately placed. Under the tree lay one present for each member of the family. Nothing costly, though it gave complete contentment. We all had a feeling that God blessed our tiny castle.

Being bilingual was another experience which made my Christmas more meaningful. It was a Feast Day and on our little hill we celebrated a special birthday. One of the main courses of our dinner consisted of a pastry called Kolac and povtica, the former being equivalent to a walnut coffee cake and the latter to our strudel. Besides these dishes, my mom made a certain type of bread that was truly symbolic for that time of year. Everything about one dwelling place expressed a time of joy and gratitude. Even the fields, the hills, the barns, the wagon wheels, the fences and hedges and the skating rinks were either capped or covered with a new blanket of snow - all of this giving us best wishes for another Christmas.

Now, in my own family circle, we chat by the fireside and talk about Christmas in other lands, rich or poor, and about those who do not understand the thoughts of what this season would be like without a tree, without laughter, without music, without friends, without a love that fills the entire household and without going to church.

At the moment, I am still obsessed by the smell of the blade of my hatchet and the chips of balsam. Merry Christmas!

Tobacco, Spitting and Spittoons

First, let me tell you that a few of the die-hard Westsiders had asked me to write about a Cue Factory which was once a part of Niles' fabulous industries. Until someone does come up with some cue history, we'll just have to wait. It has been said that way back, there was a gang called the "bad guys" of the Westside. It would be interesting to find out who they really were.

Now about the tobacco craze. Back in my era, most boys wore knickers and tennis shoes, which, by the way, were completely laced. And the girls, of course, wore dresses. All of us loved to play ball and when we heard that the big leaguers would be in town, most of us would go to the ball diamond to watch them play. It was so competitive to see various towns play each other. It was at these games that I found some food for thought for today's story.

During these games, I was absolutely intrigued by our pitcher's mannerisms. After a while, I finally discovered why his mouth would shift from one side to the other. He was chewing tobacco, I learned, and the pitcher's mound I had imagined, was splattered with tobacco juice.

Times really haven't changed that much with the chewing bit, as many of today's ball players chew some form or tobacco even though the health experts frown upon the idea.

My father chewed and smoked Peerless and today, I wonder why he ever chose that potent blend. I had a brother, too, that chewed the stuff. I remember some years back while we visited him at his home by the shores of Lake Superior, he said, "When you get back to the big city, see if you can find me some Peerless." Not only is his favorite tobacco gone, so is he. He was 89.

I can still envision that pitcher on the mound spittin' just before he delivered the ball. He was a classic standing there staring at the catcher, the batter, and then came the ptuie! At the moment, I truly wish that I remembered his name, as that would have added just a little something extra to my story. I do know, however, that this tall lanky guy left me with a lasting impression. I'm sure there were others at the ball park that were equally as impressed.

I do recall being with my father and uncle visiting a local saloon at Calumet, Michigan where most of the gents that lined the bar were sporting their mustaches and chewing their favorite blend or smoking it which in most cases, was good ol' Peerless. Being in a saloon, you might have known that there were a couple of spittoons or cuspidors that were fixtures for this kind of place. If those who spat were on target, you could hear the ptuie as well as that certain ring of the spittoon! Sometimes there would even be a contest to see who could spit the furthest. There were many that missed and today I just can't picture anyone getting paid to clean up the mess!

Living around and by so many copper fields, I used to see the miners with their lunch buckets tucked under their arms walking to the mines chewin' and spittin'.

I knew that lumberjacks were champion spitters. Since their work usually took place during the winter months, you'd often see telltales of tobacco juice in the snowbanks.

Deer hunters would also exercise their spitting rights and if there was snow on the ground, they'd always find you.

Back in the good ol' days, it seemed that everybody chewed. I remember the day when a fly got into one of my professor's mouth while he was chewing.

When we were kids, most of us would imitate our elders smoking the flowery Indian tobacco and this is how some of us continued with the real stuff.

Another ideal spot for tobacco chewing was at the General Store where the guys would not only spend the time of day shooting the breeze, but they'd shop, wait for the mail, tell stories and spit in one of the corner cuspidors. If you have never been in such a place, you have missed a lot of learnin'.

Some time ago, I asked one of my teaching confreres, "Where do you spit?" He grinned when he said, "I don't!" On many occasions, I would see him picking at his snuff box.

Ol' timers will tell you that in order to be a good spitter, you need some strong front teeth. May be that those who spit cherry pits have a different angle.

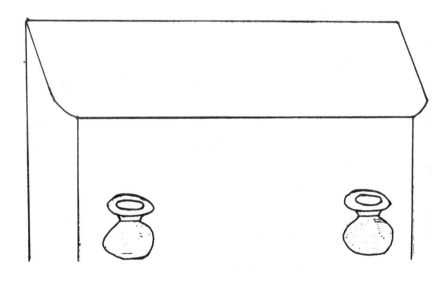

Spittin' & Spittoons

Hazelnuts, Thimbleberries and Chokecherries

It wasn't too long ago that we visited a saloon in Calumet watching a tobacco spittin' contest. While you were there, you learned that many hit their target, the spittoon and you also learned that there were many who missed. Now I am going to tell you why so many missed and it's simply that some didn't have strong front teeth. Back in the ol' days, many men would crack the hazelnuts with their teeth and in the process of doing so, they would break their teeth.

Just in case you do not know what hazelnuts are, and I have a feeling that many in these parts never saw any, so why don't we take another jaunt up Superior way and look for some?

It's just about time to pick these goodies but I must tell you that it's an unpleasant chore. The hazelnut tree looks very much like an overgrown shrub. On it, you will find a rare delicacy. Picking them is another story as they are covered by a bur or prickly growth. The fruit of the tree grows in clusters and its leaves are oval shaped with toothed edges. I suggest that you wear gloves.

I can still hear my mother telling me, "It's time to take the gunny sack, sonny, and head for the hazelnut bush." She said this in her native tongue which was Croatian and that was the first language I learned. Since all the nuts had that nasty covering, they had to be shucked and this I would do by hitting the sack of nuts over a large boulder. When I came home, I picked out the finished product.

All the nuts were put away until it was time for holiday baking. During this time, these precious meats were used in my mother's sweet breads or placed in her special pastry called Povatica. By the way, I did manage to stash a couple handfuls before my mother hid them! I still have most of my teeth!

From one delicacy to another, namely, the thimbleberry. Here's another fruit that most people in Southwestern Michigan are not aware of. Frankly, I do not know where this berry is grown other than in the Copper Country. People have told me that it may be the copper veins underground that are responsible for their growth. The plants are usually found in rocky woods, thickets and on shores. It has large maple-like leaves which are almost of velvety texture. It has a hair-like growth on the veins of the underside. You will find that the leaf has three or four toothed lobes. Once the plant is fully developed, it serves as a ground cover in open woods. Around June or July it bears a snowy white flower and by late August, the plant will produce a rich colorful red berry that is tart in flavor and not too tasty when eaten raw. The meat of the berry is very juicy and when made into jelly or jam, it would make any pastry gourmet take the next flight to fetch some for his next pastry.

Being that they are so colorfully red, I have no doubt in my mind that the early Indian used it for some of their ritualistic dances. They also used the fresh thimbleberry in their cakes which was then dried. The younger tender shoots were eaten as a vegetable.

By the way, should you ever wish to have a recipe for thimbleberry jam or jelly, don't hesitate to ask and I'll even "throw in" a place where to look for them!

Now every gourmet likes to serve some rare vintage for his guests. May I suggest a goblet of one of Copper Country's finest wild wines, the chokecherry?

While we're still out in the wilds, let me point out one of the wild American cherries called chokecherries which when ripe, has a purple-black color and is sour in taste and sensitively dry hence its name, chokecherry. It grows in clusters and the tree has leaves similar to that of our common Elm. Besides man, there are other beings that enjoy these morsels, namely, the black bears and it's their droppings that will tell you that this is their country, too!

The wild pink cherry is also a favorite of wine makers. I am sure that the Indians didn't bypass this either, especially its cousin, the chokecherry.

My dad and uncle were great connoisseurs of wines. I would often watch them at work being so methodical and meticulous about this business. And when it was time to test their labors, it was gusto all the way. Bon appetite!

Joy and Fright

Let's go back to the year 1926. The land then is the same as it is today, it's scenic, it's beautiful. Only the roads have changed. Unquestionably, the log that I saw in this old pond is still there. At any rate, I wish to take you back that many years to the region known as the Keweenaw Peninsula and awesome Lake Superior. We are all going on a camping and trout fishing expedition. I call it this because it is a five mile hike to our campsite. At the moment, I am looking at a detailed map of Keweenaw County in the Upper Peninsula of Michigan. If you're really interested in this trip, try to locate a map of the U.P. Now, locate Highway 41 going toward Copper Harbor. When you reach the junction past Delaware location called Bete Grise and Lac La Belle, stop and get your bearings. Just forget about knowing how to pronounce those names. Both of these places are located on the eastern shores of Lake Superior.

I do want you to know that this is an expedition and not a lazy afternoon boat trip fishing with your favorite Bud! Believe me, you're going to rough it. This isn't the 90s, this is back in the 20s when we didn't have any Coleman products, no sleeping bags, no tents, no chain saws, no frozen foods and, for that matter, not even a cooler. Now that I told you all the rotten things about going camping, are you still interested?

My father, who was an avid outdoorsman, is really the one who engineered this trout fishing mania and I have him to thank for paving my way for a life of adventure. If my memory serves me right, there were five of us on this excursion. I recall my father loading up his Model T with a couple of axes and saws, some warm clothing as the evenings near the shores of Lake Superior were very cool. The biggest order of the day was the food stuffs which consisted of homemade bread and jellies, hot dogs, ring bologna and beans. The pans were placed in a box made for the running board of the car. My brother and I were trout die-hards in the crew so we took along two telescopic fishing poles. Where they were made in the U.S., I do not know but they were on the market.

We drove to the spot where we would eventually begin our hike. Incidentally, my father let me take along my shepherd pup. Each person had something to carry. This truly became an expedition. I remember being very fond of the so called "government pole" used for fishing in small creeks. I usually carried with me some hooks and line which later I would wrap around the end of a long Tag Alder branch. Each time that I finished my fishing, I broke the end of that branch and wound the line around that piece and carried it in my overalls' pocket until my next trip.

Knowing that this would be my first night away from home, I must admit that I was a bit lonesome. The trail that we took was first made by some lumberjacks who at one time skidded fallen trees through this dense forest. Whenever the brush became thick, we'd blaze the trail so that we could see it on our return trip. My father knew that somewhere on this trail would be an abandoned lumber camp. It was called Bushnell's Camp. As we walked along, we'd stop for a few minutes by the tiny spring-fed creeks and try our luck at some brookies. The few that we caught were not lunkers but they were truly native.

We learned that the path that we were walking on was a trapper's paradise as we found several on our way. My shepherd pup found one, too. This is when I first learned how to release a trap. In the case of the pup, they put a stick in its mouth to release its paw.

There it was, Bushnell's Camp! I truly wish that I had some photos to show you this ol' lumber camp. All that was standing were three sides of the building. which was originally made from logs. I didn't know what a camp was until many years later so let me give you a better picture of one. A camp that was in operation had several men working for the company. These hard working men stayed at the camp, they ate and slept there and every camp had a cook who took great care of those men. Everything was homemade and the food was superb. I know that to be a fact as I stopped in at one and had some coffee and a piece of pie. It was early afternoon when we arrived and the sky was a little overcast which was most ideal for trout fishing. I knew that Copper Creek was just below our campsite so I made a mad dash plowing through some tall grass and thistle and dropped my line in this darkish brown creek. The trout that I had caught and those that were already caught earlier were enough to feed the tired crew. These speckled trout were prepared in a skillet over an open fire.

While I was at "play", a lean-to was being made for our evening's sleep. This was another of my first, namely, a lean-to. The spot was a good one to be sure as it was away from any falling timber. For those that enjoyed coffee, it was made in an open pot over the hot coals. You talk about some delicious java!

Now that I am presently so far removed from this unforgettable location, I usually sit and reminisce about the things and places that I saw when I was just a kid. I still have this map beside me and I am looking at Mt. Bohemia, Mt. Houghton, Breakfast Lake and, of course, Copper Creek. All of which I almost touched as we made that overnight trek. I still envision myself walking along that trodden path made not only by lumbermen, but perhaps by copper mining prospectors as copper veins were most everywhere in the Keweenaw Peninsula. There was much tall grass that I sneaked through and many windfalls that I easily jumped over. I remember cupping my hands to drink water from the many springs. I also remember hearing the noises of the tiny creatures searching for their nightly tidbits and the calls of the horned owls put a chill in my spine. I thought of this lumber camp in its "hayday" the working horses resting for the night, the men playing poker and having their snacks just before hitting the sack. How can I forget my father and uncle spoofing me about the man-eating creatures that roamed the night. The most consoling and exhurberant feeling was when all of us sat by the campfire talking, listening, laughing and looking at each other's face being lit by the flames. We each had a place to lie down in our big lean-to and just before I went to sleep that scary night, I took one more look at the star studded sky. I was firmly convinced that the silence of the forest was truly most rewarding.

The stories that I have written today are by no means fictitious they have all happened to me in the late 20s and early 30s. Believe me, it wasn't any popularity contest nor were we out there for any trophies or lunker fishing. This camping trip was indeed primitive and I want to assure you that if I could go back that many years, I'd start tomorrow and so would many others.

When I scout for trout streams today I often come upon old campsites that deer hunters use annually and these would always be near some stream. When I do see them, I just like to look around the way they pitch their camp. I especially notice the sleeping "bunks" made out of hay or straw; their roughly made places of eating, their crude looking privies or would you rather have me call them outhouses? Those who go for this style of camping, hurrah for our side!

Now for the thriller and hair-raiser! You remember reading a few minutes ago when I was eight and side-stepping live traps on Bushnell's Trail, now I am 15 and the know-it-all type. We had those kind even back in the 30s. There were about six of us that went on this trout excursion. Just to acquaint you first with this particular terrain, let's continue on Highway 41 toward Copper Harbor. From the eagle's keen eye sight, we're looking down from Brockway Mt. Drive which is Highway 26 at an old abandoned and overgrown trail once used by the U.S. Army. To this day, it is still called by many the Ol' Military Trail extending some 14 miles from Fort Wilkins at Copper Harbor to Eagle Harbor to the west. The soldiers presumably used this as a daily maneuver. There was talk at the time about a possible Indian uprising and hence, the building of Fort Wilkins. At any rate, we camped at about the middle of the trail which would make it equidistant from both harbors. We were right by an old Beaver Pond and this is its present day marking. It was during that night that we heard the darndest commotion going on besides the usual splashing made by the beaver's tail. I was told later that we were in the heart of bear country. We broke camp the next morning, not because of Mr. Bruin, but we looked for "greener pastures." We moved closer to Copper Harbor to a stream called Garden Brook. It is still there just below the Keweenaw Golf Course. We were told that there were several dams just west on the same trail. Those of you who walked the wilds of Michigan and caught speckled trout, you would not believe the bonanza we hit at these beaver ponds! The fish that we had caught we fried over an open fire. Need I say more? This was some lunch! We rested a while under some trees before we gave it another try.

You'll have to pardon me for taking you away from the climax of my story but some friends of ours just called and told us that they were on their way to the Copper Country and I knew that in a day or two, they will be within inches of the ol' trail and a few hundred yards from the most horrifying experience of my life.

How many times have you heard people say that black bears are harmless, they won't bother you and all those other untruths? I wish to tell you most emphatically that I am firmly convinced that a bear is a wild beast and certainly can become ferocious and don't let any one tell you otherwise.

Right after our siesta, we all returned in single file toward the ponds we fished earlier. Along the trail, there were Tag Alders and small grassy clearings. It was at one of these spots that my brother spotted two-two month old bear cubs pawing each other. He yelled out, "Hurry, come over here." Within a half minute or so, we stood and watched the "call of the wild" and I was the closest to this spectacle. Yes, I touched them, when to my right, out of the Tag Alder brush and with a ferocious growl, charged the she-bear and headed straight toward me. I froze momentarily and then realized that she meant business. In seconds, I backed off and this is when she stood up and took over frothing at the mouth making her fangs clearly visible. With one forearm, she motioned for her little ones to skiddoo and with the other, she dared our next move with claws extended. Today, I just can't believe that a bear could be anything but dangerous. I want you to remember that!

Biologists tell that bears give birth to their young in midwinter and you will see the cubs with their mother roaming around in May or so. Should you be roaming anywhere in bear country, be aware of that. The cubs will always make it known to their mother that strangers are around. Some years ago in the vicinity of Newberry, Michigan, a man was leisurely walking along a trail when a bear mauled him. He survived to tell his story.

I must tell you that since my close encounter with the master of Michigan's forests, I have never returned to Garden Brook though I have been tempted. On this 28th day of June 1990, the Brook still meanders across Highway 41 and enters Lake Superior some two or three miles downstream. If you have never seen a bear in the wilds, that's the place to go. Happy viewing! Then come tell about your heroics!

Ever vigilant!

Her majesty, the Queen
and her two small subjects
in the wilds of Michigan

Passage Across the Straits of Mackinac

We're back in Indian country again but we're treading on peaceful terrain. All hostilities have ceased to be and only the Chippewas and some of their in-laws, the French, have made their roots in this place of many wars.

Once the canoes of the Indian tribes zigzagged the dangerous currents of Lakes Michigan and Huron carrying war cargo and precious beaver pelts that no doubt excited the anxious traders located either at the northern or southern end of the Straits. All this came to pass during the seventeenth and eighteenth centuries. Since then, transportation across these waters has become a big and lucrative business.

People from both peninsulas wanted to see other parts of the world besides their own. They wanted to travel and for this reason, man built boats and ships not only to accommodate travelers but also their automobiles. These boats were called car ferries and in due time, ferries were made to haul freight cars and passenger trains.

It is very likely that many people from this region have never had the opportunity to ride a ferry boat in Michigan. As of the writing, there is still a railroad and car ferry that is in operation from Ludington, Michigan to Kewaunee, Wisconsin.

Back in the 30s and 40s, the Duluth South Shore Railroad Line had a run that originated at Detroit and stopped at Mackinaw City to board the railroad ferry, called the Chief Wawatam. After reaching St. Ignace, the passenger train was then unloaded to continue on its journey to the Copper Country. I certainly have fond memories of traveling this distance and since this was a steam engine operated by coal, all passengers at the end of this trip smelled like coal cinders.

I thought I'd relate this event as I know there are many railroad people still living in this whistle town.

At this point in my story, I would like to tell you about life on some of these carriers. While being a resident of this area, I used to see ferries leave this dock and other ships come in. I knew many of the crew that worked on the Vacationland, the City of Munising, the City of Cheboygan and the City of Petoskey. These were the Michigan State Ferries that made their daily runs. The Chief Wawatam was something special. She was strong and bulky. I'm sure that she weathered many a storm on the gale-swept Straits. Its sailors would often tell stories about their dangerous voyages. The car ferries, too, had their many problems fighting the high seas.

The Michigan State Ferries were indeed a proud fleet operated by proud engineers and deck hands. Believe me, these seamen had their work cut out for them especially during the raging storms. Their biggest test was in the middle of their voyage where the currents were the most treacherous and severest. During this perilous course, they would often sail quite close to Great Lakes freighters hauling grain, copper or iron to southern ports and steel mills. Had you been on the ferries on these hectic days, it would be frightening to see the passing freighters bucking the tumultuous swells. Maybe, perhaps, exciting to those who love the sea.

One way passage to either mainland, namely, the Upper or Lower Peninsula took approximately 45 minutes. I recall this one evening as a passenger on one of the ferries, together with our bowling team, headed for the confines of the Goldfront, a recreational center at Cheboygan. The trip to Mackinaw City was pleasant but on our return trip, there were moments that I shall long remember. We rocked and swayed with the Mackinac Straits tradewinds. I remember sipping fresh hot coffee with my companions and the ship's crew just to ease our tension. This may have been the first time that I ever saw chain smokers. Now to land this ship was certainly no easy task. To begin with, the ferry had to be put in reverse in order for the cars to be driven out. We did touch land with a bang, hitting the pilings and tires that outlined the dock.

Winter in and around these parts of the Great Lakes was, at times, extremely vicious. There was no water to be seen as now it was covered solidly with three or four feet of ice. The ships were still on course but they maneuvered slowly and cautiously. Some of these ferries became ice breakers and more or less paved the way for other ships. However, there were days when the Coast Guard Ice Breaker, the Mackinaw, would come to the rescue of a ferry locked in an ice jam. Since some people were stranded, they either walked to the mainland, or were taken by sleighs. I was told that the food was good and plentiful during their stay on ship. There was no need to huddle as the ship was comfy and cozy.

I believe this was the first time that I ever saw a sled pulled by a team of huskies headed for the Big Turtle's Back, Mackinac Island. I watched the driver and team as they left land and drove across the snow covered ice until the falling snow and wind hurt my eyes. Many of these brave souls were Indians or of French-Indian descent.

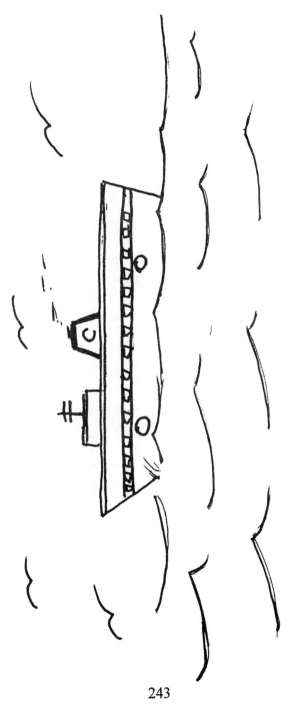

The Ferry Cheboygan hauling its cargo
against the wind and currents

World's Wonder

Last week, we traveled on the Mackinac Straits Ferries weathering the winds of the four seasons. We marveled at the way these ships sailed, so beautifully and majestically across the blue waters of Lake Michigan and Huron. We also talked about the Indians still blazing ice trails to Mackinac Island. We pictured the Duluth South Shore steaming through the meadows of Luce and Schoolcraft Counties.

The early French explorers, Jean Nicolet and Etienne Brule along with the Jesuit Missionaries making new paths and christianizing the roaming Indian tribes certainly would have stood in awe to watch ships sailing across the water that once became their nemesis.

There was much talk about building another wonder of the world to build a bridge spanning the two peninsulas. All these speculations now materialized. In the course of many years, there just had to be a meeting of the minds to come up with an ingenious plan. The man who masterminded this colossal superstructure was one of New York's prolific engineers by the name of David Steinman.

To begin this miracle, a causeway had to be constructed. This was a raised roadway projecting into the Great Lakes similar to the continental divide. This piece of land extended a mile or so into the open water. Shortly after its making, the public was permitted to either walk or drive part way to its dead end. I must tell you that this was exciting and, of course, I didn't hesitate to get as close as I possibly could to the causeway's end. It was so good to feel the Straits breezes and even getting a splash of some ice cold water. I stood there for a while and looked south across four miles of deep waters. My thoughts were so small compared to what was to be in a matter of a few short years.

The biggest obstacle to building this wonder was not so much its astronomical cost but rather the elements of nature, the unpredictable currents, the gale-force winds, the ice and snow. Anyone who has ever crossed this magnificent piece of engineering will attest to what Mother Nature can do during one of her mean moments.

Since the bridge now became a reality, the heads of state had to come up with a plan of their own, namely, what to do with the State Ferries. Somehow, somewhere they all had to put to rest. The City of Cheboygan was placed at Washington Island where it became a barge for potato storage and processing. This was a drastic change from its original design. The City of Munising was also reduced to a barge. The City of Petosky was scrapped to lay along the shores of Lake Erie in N.E. Ohio. All the power horses that carried tons of freight and human cargo have disappeared. For now, one has to go back some 34 years during the big game season when you would see several miles of waiting autos that eventually would be loaded for their trip across to the Upper Peninsula. The days of ferry travel have passed and only those who have driven over their ramps can now sit and reminisce about their glory.

It took four years to complete the construction of the Mackinac Bridge. The structure, in essence, was not built elsewhere, namely, at the quarry shops and mills in Pennsylvania, Ohio and Michigan and all parts assembled at the two Great Lakes. It is rather intriguing to note that the steel cables used in its building were long enough to circle the earth twice. Its builders used five million rivets, one million bolts and eighty-five thousand blueprints. This extraordinary achievement was made up of cofferdams, caissons supporting towers and roadbed. The world's largest suspension bridge measured 8,344 feet. The towers measure 550 feet above the surface of the water and the base is set in 220 feet of water. Story has it, though not official, that six workers had perished during its construction either by accident or natural causes.

Those of us who have crossed this span in the heat of summer have seen maintenance men either painting or doing whatever had to be done. There were others we did not see as well. They were the state's courageous deep-sea divers checking for chipped caissons caused by the annual ice flows.

Konteeka, our Indian environmentalist, was not especially pleased at first regarding what the white man has done to his beautiful world. All this while, I had a feeling that he, together with his braves, had been watching all that had come to pass the autos, the trains, the boats and the thousands of people that used his land and sea. But Konteeka was beginning to feel glad that the waters became clean and that the earth around him was once again beautified. They raised their hands and liked what they saw towering into the sky. They all proclaimed, "Our forefathers would like this very much!"

Some of the people who helped me gather detailed information of Michigan's Big Mac are William Radigan, who authored The Straits of Mackinac, and our engineer, David Steinman in collaboration with John T. Nevill, who wrote The Miracle Bridge at Mackinac.

Mighty Mac

MacDonald's Lumber Camp

Lumbering was one of the Upper Peninsula's great industries dating as far back as 1832. The places that flourished in this particular trade were Escanaba, Menominee, Masistique and Ontonagon. There were others, too, that boasted about their boom. Lumberjacks at Seney in Schoolcraft County and those at Trout Lake in Chippewa County shipped their logs by rail.

I have always wanted to know more about the life of one whose job it is to fell trees and yell, "Timber!" In the course of my travels throughout the regions of Upper Michigan, I did have an occasion to stop in at one of the lumber camps for a cup of coffee and talk with the chief cook and, of course, with that cup of java goes a delicious piece of homemade pie. Just sitting in the camp's kitchen and smelling what was being prepared on the cook stove for supper was something that I had long remembered. This was back in the late 40s and I can still picture the chef throwing another piece of wood in the stove's fire. I'm sure that these words will bring a smile on the faces of those who once stood by these cooking treasures.

I had the good fortune of visiting my friend, Bernard MacDonald, from Buffalo, New York who was the grandson of one of Mackinac County's great lumberjacks. But before we get into the crosscut sawing bit, let me tell you first about this part of New York. This was once the home of the Tuscarora and Seneca Indian tribes. I had to get through this Indian Country to get my story about lumbering in Mackinac County. There were all sorts of Indian names throughout this part of New York such as Cayuga, Lackawana, Chautauqua, Cheektawaga, Iroquois and Tonawanda. I am sure that these strange sounding names meant many things to many people. I am glad that in my search for pioneering lumbering, I was also fortunate to have treaded on the paths of the early Indian chiefs.

Bernard MacDonald was a native of Mackinac County and, as a young man, he sailed the Great Lakes on many of the ore carriers. Henry Wadsworth Longfellow once called this piece of land the Land of Hiawatha. After spending some time on the lakes, he decided to settle in Buffalo, New York where he joined forces with the Mounted Sheriff Department for Erie County, New York.

During my many visits to Upper Michigan, I would often stop at MacDonald Rapids to cast my fly for a scrappy trout and so on my next visit with Mr. Mac, I finally asked him, "Were these rapids by any chance named after him?" He gave me a very quick answer, "You bet!" "That was my grandfather's place all right." This is when he gave me a true picture of a lumbercamp.

The work of a lumberjack in the early 1900s and later took place during the winter months as the snow on the ground facilitated the skidding and swamping of logs into the frozen Carp River. Only during the spring thaw were the logs then swept by the river's current downstream into Lake Huron. The timber was then picked up by tugs and transported either by ship or train to other parts of the Midwest. Sometimes, the logs were taken to a local sawmill for cutting into various sizes. The kind of wood that was taken was soft pine and red cedar.

A typical lumber camp consisted of a bunkhouse, a cook camp, a smoke house and a barn where the draft horses were bedded for the night. Speaking of domestic animals, I find it most enjoyable to walk into a horse and cow barn during the coldest winter nights. There's just something about the warmth of an animal shelter. Picture this in a barn of a lumber camp where the big and sturdy horses spent the night when just a few hours before they had pulled and skidded logs over the snow-covered paths of the forest. During the day, too, the horses pulled sleighs that were stacked 20 feet high. The pulling distance was not very far but it was indeed a dangerous one.

As you looked in back of the camp, you would see cords of firewood that the lumberjacks cut for the cook and potbelly stoves. The smell of maple, oak, pine and birch was most inviting. Birch bark was often used to start the camp fires. You might have guessed that the privy somewhere in the back was also an important fixture.

The smoke house was truly unique as this was the place where the workers hung hams, slabs of bacon, lake trout and whitefish all of which had been soaking in brine house before. Certain woods were used for this smoking process. I believe "gusto" would be the word as you walked by this small, brown stained house!

My friend goes on to say that his grandfather owned the camp at the rapids and was very strict with his men especially dealing with horses. He would often reprimand them for whipping the horses. Mac recalls living in a cabin near the camp one winter with his family and it was during that time that he had a close look at the life of these sinewy men. He remembers riding a sulky back and forth from St. Ignace, a distance of 15 miles. He had a big grin on his face when he told me about the day he fished through the floor of the smoke house which extended over the river. His grandfather always told him to use a pin for a hook, and I guess with good results.

There was a roothouse underneath the floor and as a young Mac did a little searching, he found some lard there which was often used as a spread over homemade bread. This was commonplace back in the 20s.

A lumberjack breakfast consisted of a stack of pancakes using sugar in place of syrup or a plate covered with ham or bacon eggs. Coffee was always on the stove from the moment he was awakened until he retired in the evening. For his lunch, there were thick sandwiches such as ham, beef or pork. For supper, which was the big meal after a hard day's work, there was usually roast beef, pork, mash potatoes and gravy. I am almost certain that venison would occasionally be on the menu since the crew lived out in the wilds even though there may have been some small restrictions on game laws. Homemade pies were always in order for each day. It really didn't matter what variety they were as any piece stuck to the ribs of these hard-working men.

"My grandfather had his own personal sleigh and a slick black horse," Mac continued. "It was told that my grandfather came to camp late one evening after visiting his friends at the local saloon. As he was approaching camp with his cutter, the horse went over a stump that was protruding from the deep snow which tipped the cutter and its rider. My grandfather wore his bear-skinned coat that night and you can imagine what he looked like in the white background. While lying in the snow slightly inebriated, his horse continued on the road back to camp." The grandson grinned all this while and he went on to say that a lumberjack was having a late cup of coffee, heard the neigh of a horse and spotted the black beauty standing outside without a rider. It was just a matter of minutes when the bunkhouse was alive with sleepy men clothed in flappy long johns. They all bolted out of the door and ran back a few hundred yards and found their boss lodged in a snowbank, somewhat dazed, but more concerned about his horse. When they returned to camp, it was more black coffee before they hit the sack.

The grandson showed me some old snapshots of the lumbercamp, his grandfather and his crew. This was back in 1918. One of the photos was about the older Mac standing by some empty wagons and looking as though he was ready to give command to a lumberjack, "All right, fellow, no whip on that horse, understand?" The other picture showed men with their horses perhaps just finishing a day's work.

Mac told me about the time when he was about eight years old, the day that he and his friends took a walk downtown by one of the saloons to see whether he could spot his grandfather. He didn't see him, but he did recognize some of the lumberjacks smoking cigars, cigarettes, chewing tobacco and spitting in cuspidors that were lined up at the front of the bar. Who knows, maybe they had a contest going on to see who could spit the furthest or just hitting their target. At camp, you would always know who chewed the most as there were telltale splashes all over the snow-covered terrain.

The sheriff from New York also described some of the tools that were used. To begin with, they had single and double edge axes along with a broad ax which was used for hewing logs that were, in turn, used for building beams. He gave me a good idea what a cant hood was used for. Crosscut saws were a must in this land of virgin timber. He also mentioned that draw knives were necessary for peeling cedar logs. He brought to mind many things that I personally had seen while traveling this beautiful peninsula. Incidentally, that cant hood we talked about was primarily used for rolling logs but it was also employed for harvesting ice that was cut on the inland lakes. I vividly recall the day that I saw a small steam engine train puffing along an old railroad bed pulling gondolas loaded with huge logs. Directly in front of the locomotive were two lumberjacks armed with shotguns looking for Partridges that may have been feeding at that time of day. At the moment, I did not know what these men were sitting on but I did tell Mac about it and he said that this was called a "cowcatcher." I am sure that there were days when this part of the train did its job. Just watching the engine coming around the bend was indeed a memorable occasion.

Why this descendent of a lumberman ever chose to patrol the streets of Buffalo, New York as a mounted Sheriff still puzzles me. He could have very well continued to sail the cold waters of the Great Lakes and while doing so, he could have had some fond memories of sailing near the mouth of the Carp River where his grandfather was once the chief of falling timber. At the moment of this writing, he still manages to steal his way to Mackinac County to capture the smell of MacDonald Rapids.

Had it not been for this seagoing officer, there are not too many of us left to tell the young minds of today about the life of a lumberjack.

It was shortly after I completed this writing that I learned about Bernard MacDonald's death on Saturday, September 22, 1990. His passing saddened me greatly, as he was not only a long time friend, but also one who has left me with priceless memories of the land that once belonged to the Chippewas. It is for this reason that I dedicate these thoughts in memory of Mac, the dancer, the sailor and Mounted Sheriff of Erie County, New York.

The passerby today will still be able to note a trace of a camp that once harbored strong draft horses and their tough and hungry masters. The visitor will also observe that the river continues to flow swiftly down towards the Huron, one of the Big Five.

The Older Mac's crew at Carp River in the '20s

Autumn Fire

There is a certain chill that accompanies the northwest winds; the air is crisp. The advent of another season has suddenly brought some climactic changes. It is fall 1992. The clouds during the next three months will become foreboding. The Canadian Honkers have been gathering up enough steam on their flyways to the south. Chain saws will be heard well into the season reminding us of what is yet to come.

There is indeed a distinct smell of falling leaves and those that have already blanketed the floors of the forests. This is truly the occasion when hunters pursue and stalk their wild game. What a memorable moment for a novice!

Unquestionably, this is the most exhilarating time of the year when Mother Nature puts on a show in living color. It appears that the trees are in some kind of contest to see what species displays the greatest splendor. Frankly, they are all magnificent. I am sure that they would all enjoy being recognized as being spectacular. But the most prominent of all would have to be the Maples. Standing right beside these beauties you will find the Birch, the Elm, the Wild Cherry, the Chokcherry, the Aspen, the Sugarplum and, finally, the Blazing Sumac. Those of you who are familiar with the forest will note that there is a bit of majesty added to the forest supreme when we include the family of the firs. It is for this reason that anyone traveling the highway of Michigan will be delighted to witness this colorful phenomenon.

To camp in the midst of color and woodland aroma are moments that you will harbor for years to come. My son, Michael, and I camped in Mackinac County in the vicinity of Cut River some 25 miles from Mackinac Bridge. The weather was in our favor for a few days and that's all that really mattered. Our trip was twofold, namely, to do a little fishing and small game hunting. Hunting deer with a bow and arrow was also on the agenda. Our score was nil but just knowing that we had touched the waters for Steelhead at the Carp and seeing and hearing drumming Partridges was indeed well worth our trip across Big Mac. And besides cruising those old CCC roads from one end to another was worth a million as it brought back some exciting memories when my Model A toured those wild forest avenues.

What an exuberant feeling it was when we returned to our campsite after some late hours of hunting. It was just about twilight when we built a fire. Believe me, that felt so good as a cold heavy dew suddenly settled over our area. We waited quite a while for a blazing hot fire but after it simmered down a bit, we readied a few tantalizing sirloin steaks and peeled some spuds. This was not all as just a short distance from the campfire, anchored in Little Brevort, were a few cans of brew. Chilled appetizers one might call them. This is what I would call real gusto!

Now comes the camaraderie of father-son talk. We both looked deep into the fire and reminisced a bit and planned for the next day's run. We checked our bearings on Mackinac County's detailed map by the light of our fire. We noted that the sky was clear and splashed with an infinite number of stars, galaxies, constellations and, of course, the moon was smiling all the while. The night was beginning to get quite cold and this is when my son threw a few more logs on the fire. Just then, one of Michigan's Horned Owls gave a hoot that echoed across a mile of towering hemlocks. Maybe this is what caused me to hit the sack for the night.

I remembered earlier in the day when we spotted a pickup truck dragging a Fir tree about the width of one of these roads which startled both of us for several hours. As a matter of fact, we talked about it by the fire wondering why would anyone be dragging a tree out in these forsaken places. It appeared as though the occupants of the truck were trying to hide some evidence of some sort. The answers came the next morning when we met two of the men who were responsible for the dragging operation. Naturally, during the day, there are a thousand tracks made by humans, animals and vehicles. It was their goal to erase all tracks so that they could find one prominent track which was that of the bear. You see, these clever operators had tracking dogs with them and once a bear track was located, then the music started! Besides learning the tricks of the hunting trade, we also learned what a fisher track looked like. It didn't take the ol' timer too long to let us know about this critter. Had we stayed with him, we probably would have been taught the history of Michigan wildlife.

I was glad that my son had a chance to see this new adventure and now that he is a student pilot, I know that in due time, he will navigate the wilds of this great state. And I know, too, that he will buzz the roads and trails along Little Brevort River. His uncle would have been quite proud as he, too, once buzzed the village of Brevort.

It was clearly seen that the autumn fire in these parts was gradually being put to rest by the cold, the frost and the wind.

I didn't particularly cherish the idea of leaving this side of Mighty Mac as this terrain, and points further north, are my roots. We were both pleased to know, though, that our return trip to Lakeview would still be flanked by autumn fires.

An Escape to the Land of Copper

So many beautiful and exciting things have already been penned about the Copper Country but I personally would enjoy having you accompany me to this place of land so richly endowed with copper veins. This is my birthplace and a place where I often camped, fished, hunted, blazed trails and searched for wild berries, such as strawberries, raspberries, blueberries and thimbleberries. And this is still the land where rock hounds search for Lake Superior agates.

Those of you out there somewhere in this great State of Michigan who are interested or have aspirations of trying to locate these precious gems, let me show you some favorite spots. But you must be patient. When I was growing up in this Superior country, I learned that the best time to look for agates is when the Great Lake would cough up some rocks after a storm. And if you're the daredevil type, you could always fight the fury of Lake Superior. Do not underestimate its madness.

Let's start looking at Seven Mile and Five Mile Points which are accessible by taking a main route from Ahmeek off Highway 41. From there, we can drive along the big lake to Eagle River. After we have combed these areas, we can proceed to Copper Falls, to Eagle Harbor and then on to Copper Harbor, the home of Fort Wilkins. Now we're headed toward Horseshoe Harbor, Keweenaw and Keystone Points. Manitou Island is also noted for this spectacular glacier rock. If you're the outdoor type and wish to camp at these place, then the wilderness awaits you.

Should you and your family choose these particular confines, then you're in for some memorable nocturnal sounds. If you're camping near some lonely lake at dusk, you'll be greeted by the screams of the loon. And if you are lucky enough, you will be charmed by the call of the Whippoorwill. The hoots of the Horned Owl will keep you awake and if this doesn't scare you, then its cousin, the Screach Owl, will make you wonder, "Why did I ever choose this sort of vacation?" The coyote's ahoooooo might startle you and if your campsite is near a beaver dam, then the splash of its tail might shake you up. Perhaps the tramping of Big Foot, the Black Bear, will force you to take note! Writing about this critter is another story as we met face to face when I was in my early teens. This all took place in the vicinity of Keweenaw Lodge.

Even after listening to the sounds of the wilderness, you did manage to get some sleep but you were awakened at a reasonable hour by a squawking Osprey as it wanted to tell you that you were now on his fishing grounds.

While you are still undecided where to go from here, let's take a five mile jaunt to Brockway Mount Drive. Once you have reached its peak, you can now use your field glasses and enjoy the sights of four inland lakes, namely, lakes Medora, or as some would prefer to call it, Mosquito Lake, Upson, Bailey, Fanny Hooe and, of course, the greatest fresh water lake in the world, Lake Superior. While you are still on top of this gigantic piece of rock, look down you will see an old beaver pond that could tell us a thousand stories. Just beside this body of water there is an overgrown military trail that was once a training area for the soldiers from Fort Wilkins at Copper Harbor.

I so vividly remember all the outings in Keweenaw County combing agate beaches, exploring trout streams and beaver dams. For the outdoor minded, there are so many trails that you could take; trails that the early lumberjacks used to skid their lumber and trails that would take you directly to their lumbercamp which in many instances would be located near some moving water. Remnants of these early work places are still found in the Bete Grise area. Other places that come to mind at the moment, that we explored in our growing up years together with our elders, were Breakfast Lake and mounts Houghton and Bohemia. All these and so much more is still there for you to explore. I am almost certain that there are many spots on this copper soil that have never been seen, touched or walked upon. Every bit of it is well worth your visit to see, touch, smell and listen to.

Montreal River, one of Keweenaw County's great trout waters, meanders through some early mining towns, such as Central, Delaware and Mandan. I remember back in the 50s when we used one of the old mining houses as deer camps. Continuing on Highway 41, you will note Iron City trail and Empire Mine trail both of which will take you to the Montreal. The headwaters of this river begin at Central and its mouth is on the southern shores of the Big Spring, Lake Superior. While you're out there somewhere off the beaten path, always be aware of small mounds that are sealed by a barbed wire fence which could be sites of early abandoned mines.

Our State's Motto translated from the Latin reads, "If you seek a pleasant peninsula, look about you." And from my personal experience, you will be absolutely exhilarated to visit this land that still has in its belly some of the richest copper veins in the world.

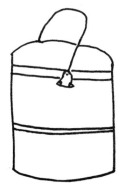

A miner's lunch bucket

Deep in the belly of the earth

261

The Drummers

This is nostalgic hunting back in the 40s and 50s when Model As and tote roads were the talk of most of Michigan's Upper Peninsula towns. When you were just a kid growing up in the tiny village of Calumet, you used to wait for your father to come home after a day's hunt whether it would be a chase after snowshoe rabbits, deer or partridge. He always did manage to return with game that was in season either feathered or furred. His love for the wilds was rather obvious as his clothes often carried the scent of the forest.

You were very proud of your father as he showed you the skills of being a hunter, and after much persuasion, you finally received the classic picture of your father, which today graces our home. It is a large photo of him standing and holding his priceless .12 gauge shotgun. Tied to his cartridge belt is a brown snowshoe hare and flanking your father's right, was a maker of forest music, his irreplaceable hound. It is for this reason that you have become such an avid hunter and admirer of the wilderness. That picture of the mighty nimrod dates back to the year 1905.

You were only in your teens when you admired your father's single barrel .12 gauge shotgun and you vowed that one day you, too, would sport a shootin' iron and bring home the "bacon." It wasn't until 1945 that you first owned a gun, a .16 gauge Springfield which, to this day, compliments your home. It seems that you went hog-wild that year as you also invested in a 30-30 Winchester rifle. Both of these firearms have given you immeasurable pleasure throughout the years.

In your many walks through the forest, you were often startled by the drumming of a partridge. Even while fly fishing at the bottom of an aspen cliff, this particular sound was very persistent. It must have been your first real experience with a drummer at work. The bird did captivate you, so much so, that you stopped fishing and sat on a nearby log and just listened. You thought for a moment that the feathered animal was within eye contact but since you were surrounded by a wall of trees, the sound baffled you.

You recall this one day when you spotted a brood of partridge chicks scrambling for cover. It was absolutely amazing how each little Pat disappear under leaves and ferns in just a matter of seconds.

Your first bird hunt took place in Mackinac County in the vicinity of Kenneth, a small railroad spur north of Moran. Frank Alich was the navigator of your hunting party. If he wasn't telling you about the good places to hunt, then he'd spend the time telling you stories about the European immigrants in their own particular dialect. You found this to be especially hilarious as you once lived in their midst and knew their ways of life. This storyteller always carried a small pad with him reminding himself about the next story or was about to record a new one that he had just heard. Your hunt was indeed a memorable one, not only for bringing down your target but also for all the big laughs as you strolled down the leaf-covered trails. You knew one thing about this guy and that was his humor. This is why you chose to remember him as being a beautiful person.

Hunting these wild and elusive birds during the peak of the fall colors is most exciting and breath-taking. At one point in your life, the Upper Peninsula was your permanent residence and you remembered all the blazed trails and the off beaten paths. You scored well on many occasions but then there were times that your gun didn't shoot straight!

In search of wild game on Michigan's tote roads from a Model A was especially unbeatable. Going out for a hunt in late afternoon and early dusk is most ideal, as this is the time of day when Ruffed Grouse pick up bits of gravel just as their cousins do back on the farm.

A sudden flash of a Pat or a Covey can be most alarming and once they're in flight, their maneuverability is unmatched. Should you ever find your target under such conditions, then you have every right to boast about your kill. How can you forget the day when you nailed one as you shot from the hip? And since it happened so many years ago, you could even come close in showing someone the exact spot.

You crept along in your prize auto this one afternoon when you noticed two Pats fighting in the roadway. It was quite a show but then your fingers became too fidgety! It may have been the same afternoon when you came upon a snowshoe sitting in the middle of the road and suddenly a bird of prey picked up its meal. Since it was getting quite late in the afternoon, you guessed the scavenger to be a horned owl. It is scenes such as these that make your trips to the forest most rewarding.

The opening day of Ruffed Grouse hunting in Mackinac County seemed to have centered around Worth's Trading Post, a tasty eatery and lively pub. Where else could you find the camaraderie of men talking about their kill and many misses?

Winter comes and all the drums cease to beat. All your feathered friends can now be seen perched on lofty bare Oaks and Maple trees. You will see them in early hours of twilight. As you snowshoe your way through woodland trails, you will note places where these game birds bury themselves in snow thus protecting their bodies from some of nature's severest elements. And if the night has left a coat of ice on the forest's floor, this spells disaster for those that plunge from their perches.

Come next fall, there will be new feathered drums to hear and a new brood to search and plan for the next tasty morsel.

Camouflage At Its Best, The Snowshoe

I guess it was your family trait that all the males would "bear arms". Since you were the youngest of the clan, it seems that it took forever for you to cradle a shotgun. You were in your twenties when you heard the call of the wilds. At the time, you lived in a small French-Indian community where hunting was a way of life.

You talked about rabbit hunting with several of your friends and they all guaranteed you an exciting hunt come late fall or early winter. There was a little snow on the ground which made excellent tracking for the two beagles that came along.

This was Carp River Country in Mackinac City. You could tell that you were with a bunch of bushmen as they knew every trail leading in and out of a twisted cedar swamp. Your buddies really showed you what snowshoe hares looked like and how they operated. There were rabbits flying all over the place up an down the ravines along this cold meandering river. This was the day that, for the first time in your life, you brought down your quarry, a white snowshoe!

These French and French-Indian people often spoke of a traditional tasty dish that they called "rabbit with gleesons" which was much similar to the American stew with dumplings. Believe me, if you never had rabbit stew, then you're in for a very special treat. From that group of jovial and happy people, you are the sole survivor of that Carp River chase.

You remember the day that you hit a small thick swamp a place you were told that was heavily populated with rabbits. All the snow that had fallen earlier in the month was now melted. Of course, this made "easy pickins'". There was no need for you to take your shotgun and, besides, you wanted to give your quarry a sportin' chance. So, your .22 rifle took care of the limit. That little pocket of hemlocks and evergreens smelled from gunpowder for the remainder of the day.

It was in the early 50s that one of the ol' timers of a small farming town gave you a hunting dog, a beagle and spaniel mix. The old gent enjoyed the outdoors but due to his ailing health, he was no longer able to hunt. As talk would have it in a tiny community, he learned that you, too, enjoyed a good rabbit hunt and since you liked his dog's company, it didn't take long for the experienced hunter to say, "Take him, he's yours."

The happy donor told you how he trained his hound while out in the field. After each kill, the owner would remove the rabbit's liver and give it to the dog. You followed these instructions to the letter. As time went on, you also learned that this dog was crazed by the smell of gunpowder. Since the hound was about a year or two old, you renamed him as Gunsmoke. And so it was that this gun-crazy beast became a buddy.

Some nice people told you about a natural bowl for rabbit hunting. The bowl, a circular swamp, was surrounded by a ridge. Your beagle was on track in just a few minutes and you found out in a hurry that this was snowshoe country. Your five hunting partners were all well posted. Now it was your dog's turn to show-off his animal instincts. None of you had too much time to visit, as what you heard coming from that wild swamp was music to a hunter's ear. The barks were getting frequent, closer and determined and suddenly this small piece of land became a war zone. When you downed your fleeing target, you knew that your irreplaceable hound would soon retrieve his chase. When he brought you his prize, you knew exactly what to do. And as soon as you gave him that liver, he was gone! Two of your friends saw this maneuver and were amazed. This was a day that you long remembered.

You became rather attached to Gunsmoke as he did toward you. You kept your arsenal in the hallway and don't think for one moment that the dog didn't know that. Your pet was an outdoor type. There was no question about that. You did let him indoors on occasion and this is when you used to torment him by reaching for your .16 gauge. You'd often say, "Let's go fella!" It knew, too, when you started to put on your huntin' togs that it was time to hit his favorite swamp. Anything that had to do with the wilds, this animal was beside himself.

As you left the house, Gunsmoke made a beeline to the Model A and waited for you to open the door and both of you were off to another search. Several inches of snow fell during the night which meant good tracking for the dog and good snowshoeing with your bear-paws. You just managed to reach the thicket and noticed that the dog was gone. He found what he was after and the music continued until you left at dusk with your limit of wild game. Trying to get your music-maker out of the bush was a futile attempt. This is when you remembered one of the instructions that came with the hound the day he was given to you. "There'll come a day", the ol' timer once said, "That you won't be able to get the critter out of the bush." So, you left your glove tucked under an evergreen and hoped that he would be there come midnight. Not only did you find him nestled by your glove, but you also had a large soup bone that he savored on his return trip home.

Early the following spring, this remarkable animal left the confines of your residence and never did return. But you do have memories of an incredible rabbit chaser and retriever.

Unforgettable Moments

There are moments in one's life when he would want the whole world to see what he had just seen. Today's story are the unforgettable moments that I wish to share with my readers.

First, it is indeed most comforting to learn that many people enjoy my stories and I must tell you that it's just as consoling writing them. The other day, our family physician spotted me and said, "You're kind of leaning toward the Upper Peninsula, aren't you?" You could have guessed that his remark put a big smile on my face. I gave him a quick answer, too, "You bet!" I'm pretty proud to tell you something about that piece of land that has copper and iron veins and, surely, about its happy people.

Today's episode takes place just a stone's throw from the frozen shores of Lake Michigan along U.S. Highway 2 some 18 miles west of Big Mac. It was extremely cold this one day in January 1959. The cold was bitter and stinging. The thermometer read minus 22°. This was nothing unusual as this was quite common in these parts especially in January.

The moon was full early that morning and its smile was worth talking about. Some new snow fell the night before just to make things a bit more wintry. It was truly a moonlit night and with the snow, one could easily pick out objects in the dark. This was the kind of night that every tree showed its shadow. This was playtime for all the snowshoe rabbits making new runways all over the place and this was the kind of night when you would have clearly heard the sounds of the forest. Some of these were absolutely eerie such as the Ahooooooooh of two coyotes answering each other's call or the hoots of owls. You could even hear their wings in flight. You also distinctly heard the snapping of tree limbs. The crackling and resounding of the ice on Lake Michigan would continue for miles, and perhaps even further, until the sound was no longer audible.

Back in '59, our home was overlooking the Great Lake and our views through the picture window were absolutely superb including the one that I so vividly recall. It was snowing a bit this one afternoon when I sighted a lone coyote headed out into the open really "carrying the mail". Behind him a short distance were four barking dogs probably the coonhound variety and they, too, weren't wasting anytime! Whether the dogs ever caught up with the varmint, I couldn't say but I did learn a day or so later who the hunter was.

There was a rap on our bedroom window about 2 a.m. on this one cold night when, Jim, my wife's brother, who at the time, lived over the next ridge, was yelling, "I need your help, hurry, they're on their way!" We talked about something like this happening, but what day, what time of day this miracle would take place, was far from our minds.

It didn't take too long to wrap ourselves in mackinaws, scarfs, caps and boots. We tore out of the house and headed through the woods toward the distress area. There was no need to lock our doors as this was the era when people were free from care. As we walked, we could hear our crunching steps until we came to this place of many births. The barn was lighted and as we walked in, we sensed the warmth of the animal kingdom. We found Jim working feverishly with his prize sow. She was in extreme labor delivering her piglets and this is when Jim demanded, "Grab hold." All three of us were greenhorns at this sort of thing. The sow grunted painfully and at each grunt, there was a newborn. The piglets actually popped out! As he handed them to us, we gently cleaned each one of them and placed them by their mother. Our big concern was that she could smother the litter. My wife and I just couldn't picture ourselves being surgical nurses. The whole procedure lasted about two hours. The whopping toll read seventeen, two runts of which did not survive.

Besides the contented sow, there were other animals looking on each giving its special sound, namely, the cow, the two horses and four other pigs. A dog and cat made the picture complete. Since this miraculous event took place in the wee hours of the morning, the animal kingdom was a bit disturbed as it, too, needed its rest. There was much straw and hay in this warm place. To this day, some 32 years later, the beautiful smell of this barn still lingers.

As the cold of winter approaches, we begin to reminisce about that miracle in the forest. We often talk about Jim, as so many others do, but he is no longer with us. His sister and I are the only two witnesses to this unforgettable moment. This scene was somewhat reminiscent of Christmas at the stable. With this final thought, come warm wishes for a Happy New Year!

Along The Ridges at Brevort Camp

Do you remember that ol' bridge crossing at Brevort River not too far from the 'Black Top?' You were about 19 then and just shot your first buck in Mackinac County and your face was as red as your jacket from dragging your prize!

How about the time when you were just about ready to take your morning stand and right before you, a doe and buck bolted in midair across a small meadow. By the time you brought the rifle to your shoulder, history had passed!

Remember the day you hunted in a pine plantation off Worth's Road and you spotted something moving and you convinced yourself that it was the legs of a deer. I guess you shot it and it disappeared like a ghost. When you returned to camp, the others listened and knew that you were mad. By the way, that pine plantation is still there and so are the many fawns and yearlings sired by that buck. You can't help recall the day that you were nicely snuggled in a slashing waiting for the company of a whitetail when instead you watched a chickadee land on the barrel of your gun.

Becoming lost in the wilds is common place during the big game hunt. It's frightening, to say the least. You found a person that was lost while you hunted one year. You listened to him and all that time he gestured with his rifle. You knew this was bad business and trying to calm him down wasn't easy. At times, he acted like a wild man.

You remember well the day you were roaming the hardwoods at Round Lake after a fresh snowfall when suddenly, you spotted a deer rubbing its head on a maple sapling. You thought then that only bucks rub their antlers on trees and from your vantage point, the animal didn't appear to have antlers. Your scope was still on the animal and you said, "Wait a minute, that's a spike!" Dragging him on the snow was like pulling a toboggan. Later that same morning, you had a chance to see a ten pointer shot by one of the natives of that area.

Your biggest buck was really not a trophy but its eight point rack was so symmetric which made you pretty proud anyway. It hit the scale at slightly over 200 pounds. Had it not been for that deer making a slosh sound in the swail below, he would have not been yours. Your head became like a swivel as there was much noise created by the stiff breeze.

The best time of the day was when all of you would get together in the cigarette smoke clouded room to play cards, drink your favorite malt, tell your story of the day, and laugh even though you weren't the winner. Yes, all of you were there somewhere on the premises. Brothers, uncles, father and two sons, a father and son, the rookie, the brothers-in-law, cousins and the many friends. Just your being there was some sort of history in the making. While you were there you saw life in the wilderness and all your pleasures were good and wholesome. This could have related to future generations.

I consider all events at any camp to be exciting and the one I am about to tell you is no exception, believe me. On the third day of the season, you decided to hunt in the vicinity of the 'Black Top' where the river made an unexpected call. You leaned your Winchester on an aspen tree within your reach. There he was, an eight pointer a mere 20 feet from your squat. You grabbed your gun, wheeled around and shot twice just to see it disappear in the pines. It was only 8:00 a.m. and still a bit dark in the bush and no one else to help where you left off. You do know, though, that in all the excitement, your hunting knife slipped off the belt and was never found. After so many years, your sharp edge must be buried under heavy mulch. When you returned to camp, did they believe you?

At any rate, all of you out there knew that your hunt ended for the day. You watched the sun sink in the western shores of Lake Michigan. You also knew that the stew was on. Better still, the makings of swiss venison steak, not just for one or two, but for a score or more. Just before supper, most of you threw your smelly jackets on the bed still rattling with live cartridges. Your clothes had that outdoor wild smell and they were to be that way until you reached your real home. The days you spent in the wilds at Brevort Camp will be long remembered and talked about for years to come. Good hunting!

What Has Come To Pass

It is my hope that you have enjoyed paging through all these words and multiple thoughts. As you have undoubtedly noted, many of my thoughts and phrases were used repititiously, as these stories were used in a newspaper series and they often referred back to other issues. However, I trust this has brought you moments of joy and satisfaction and perhaps even a bit of information which otherwise would have been unanswered..

As you easily may have surmised, that I thoroughly enjoyed being with and speaking with people and have certainly enjoyed, and continue to enjoy, the confines of my state.

I began our tour in this remarkable city of Four Flags once harboring the early fur traders and French missionaries. Today, as I cross the city's bridges, overlooking the mighty St. Joseph River, I still envision a fleet of canoes being paddled by blackrobes, traders and the Potawatomis, who hurried home to show-off their day's kill of wild game.

In the course of your reading, I have taken you to the land of Hiawatha, which the poet, Henry Wadsworth Longfellow, once portrayed in one of his many poems. And while following the trails of Michigan's dense forests, I am sure that I crossed a path that Ernest Hemingway brushed leading to his favorite bend in the river that teemed with scrappy brook trout. Throughout this great state of ours, I could not escape the thought of giving you a panoramic view of a part of Henry Thoreau's world. Somehow, I have a feeling that another one of America's poets, Ralph Waldo

Emerson, by name, would have been thrilled to pen something spectacular about our Great Lakes State.

Since I first began to record my thoughts, several of my characters have now reached their eternal reward. As mentioned in my previous segments, I am indeed fortunate to have captured the fleeting moments and memories of people who have toiled and labored in the deep South, people who possessed expertise in medicine, people that have made this a great railroad city, people who excelled in the political arena, and people that showed us the ways of producing much fruit. Fortunate, indeed, to have spoken to people in years past that stood at the helm of ore freighters and ferries sailing the Straits of Mackinac.

To end my collection of varied stories, I am somewhat saddened, however, that I have never had the opportunity to walk the paths of my ancestors, nor spoken to anyone of our clan that currently reside across the high seas.